PowerShell and Python Together

Targeting Digital Investigations

Chet Hosmer

Apress®

PowerShell and Python Together: Targeting Digital Investigations

Chet Hosmer
Longs, SC, USA

ISBN-13 (pbk): 978-1-4842-4503-3   ISBN-13 (electronic): 978-1-4842-4504-0
https://doi.org/10.1007/978-1-4842-4504-0

Managing Director, Apress Media LLC: Welmoed Spahr
Acquisitions Editor: Susan McDermott
Development Editor: Laura Berendson
Coordinating Editor: Rita Fernando

Cover designed by eStudioCalamar

Cover image designed by Freepik (www.freepik.com)

Distributed to the book trade worldwide by Springer Science+Business Media New York, 233 Spring Street, 6th Floor, New York, NY 10013. Phone 1-800-SPRINGER, fax (201) 348-4505, e-mail orders-ny@springer-sbm.com, or visit www.springeronline.com. Apress Media, LLC is a California LLC and the sole member (owner) is Springer Science + Business Media Finance Inc (SSBM Finance Inc). SSBM Finance Inc is a **Delaware** corporation.

For information on translations, please e-mail rights@apress.com, or visit http://www.apress.com/rights-permissions.

Apress titles may be purchased in bulk for academic, corporate, or promotional use. eBook versions and licenses are also available for most titles. For more information, reference our Print and eBook Bulk Sales web page at http://www.apress.com/bulk-sales.

Any source code or other supplementary material referenced by the author in this book is available to readers on GitHub via the book's product page, located at www.apress.com/9781484245033. For more detailed information, please visit http://www.apress.com/source-code.

Printed on acid-free paper

To the latest addition of our family – "Cousin Vinny" – one of the sweetest, very loving, and curious Yellow Labs ever, who constantly interrupts our daily lives in the most wonderful ways.

Table of Contents

About the Author ix

About the Technical Reviewer xi

Acknowledgments xiii

Introduction xv

Chapter 1: An Introduction to PowerShell for Investigators................1

A Little PowerShell History...2

How Is PowerShell Used Today? 3

How Do You Experiment with PowerShell? 3

    Navigating PowerShell ISE 3

    PowerShell CmdLets 7

    What Is a CmdLet?...7

    Introduction to Some Key CmdLets 8

Challenge Problems: Investigative CmdLets to Explore 18

    Challenge One: Executing a "Find" Based on File Extension....................18

    Challenge Two: Examining Network Settings 19

    Challenge Three: Examining Firewall Settings 20

    Challenge Four: Your Chance to Explore 20

Summary...20

Chapter 2: PowerShell Pipelining 23

What Is CmdLet Pipelining? 23

    Example 1: Get-Service 23

    Example 2: Get-Process...27

Adding a Transcript to Track Your Activities 37

Challenge Problem: CmdLet Experimentation...41

Summary..43

Chapter 3: PowerShell Scripting Targeting Investigation 45

Basic Facts About PowerShell Scripts 46

Example 1: The EventProcessor PowerShell Script...46

    EventLog CmdLets..47

    Retrieving More Specific Eventlog Information 49

    Creating the Script..50

    EventProcessor Get-Help Result...62

    EventProcessor Script Execution..66

    Resulting Directory...67

    HTML Output Report 67

Remote Access 68

Example 2: USB Device Usage Discovery..70

    Create the Script...72

    USBAcquire Script Execution..83

    USBAcquire Get-Help Result...84

Challenge Problem: Create File Inventory List with Hashes...............................85

Summary..86

Chapter 4: Python and Live Investigation/Acquisition 89

What Is "By Example"?...90

    Directing PowerShell with Python 91

    Launching PowerShell CmdLets from Python 94

    Creating a System Files Baseline with PowerShell and Python 97

    Overview of Python Execution with PowerShell 117

Challenge Problem: Perform Remote Script Execution 118

Summary 119

Chapter 5: PowerShell/Python Investigation Example 121

Enable PowerShell Remoting 122

Gathering and Analyzing Remote Evidence 126

Invoking Remote Access 130

Building a PowerShell Script for DnsCache Acquisition 131

Python Script and PowerShell CacheAquire Script 136

Overview of Client DNS Cache Acquisition and Search 144

Challenge Problem: Multiple Target Computer DNSCache Acquisition 144

Summary 145

Chapter 6: Launching Python from PowerShell 147

Reversing Roles from PowerShell to Python 147

    Examine the PowerShell Script 148

    Examine the Corresponding Python Script 149

    Executing the Combined PowerShell to Python Scripts 150

Extracting Possible Proper Names from Text Documents 150

    Examine the PowerShell Script 151

    Examine the Corresponding Python ProperNames Script 153

    Executing the Combined PowerShell to Python ProperNames Scripts 162

Extracting EXIF Data from Photographs 164

    PowerShell Script 164

    pyGeo.py Python Script 166

    Executing the Combined PowerShell to Python exifxtract Scripts 177

Summary 178

Chapter 7: Loose Ends and Future Considerations 181

Loose Ends..181

Future Considerations 186

Summary..187

Appendix A: Challenge Problem Solutions..............................189

Chapter 1: Investigative CmdLets to Explore 190

    Challenge One: Executing a "Find" Based on File Extension.....................190

    Challenge Two: Examining Network Settings 192

    Challenge Three: Examining Firewall Settings 193

Chapter 2: CmdLet Experimentation 194

Transcript of Commands and Responses.......................................195

Chapter 3: Create File Inventory List with Hashes 203

    Sample PowerShell Script Output 206

    HTML Screenshots..206

Chapter 4: Perform Remote Script Execution 208

    Example A: Acquire Remote Processes from PLUTO....................................209

    Example B: Acquire Remote Services from PLUTO 210

    Example C: Acquire Remote IP Configuration from PLUTO 211

Chapter 5: Multiple Target Computer DNSCache Acquisition 212

Index...213

About the Author

Chet Hosmer is the founder of Python Forensics, Inc., a nonprofit organization focused on the collaborative development of open-source investigative technologies using Python and other popular scripting languages. Chet has been researching and developing technology and training surrounding forensics, digital investigation, and steganography for decades. He has made numerous appearances to discuss emerging cyber threats, including National Public Radio's *Kojo Nnamdi Show*, ABC's *Primetime Thursday*, and *ABC News* (Australia). He has also been a frequent contributor to technical and news stories relating to cybersecurity and forensics with IEEE, *The New York Times*, *The Washington Post*, Government Computer News, Salon.com, and *Wired* magazine.

Chet is the author of *Defending IoT Infrastructures with the Raspberry Pi* (Apress, 2018), *Passive Python Network Mapping* (Syngress, 2015), *Python Forensics* (Syngress, 2014), and *Integrating Python with Leading Computer Forensics Platforms* (Syngress, 2016). He coauthored *Data Hiding* (Syngress, 2012) with Mike Raggo and *Executing Windows Command Line Investigation* (Syngress, 2016) with Joshua Bartolomie and Rosanne Pelli.

Chet serves as a visiting professor at Utica College in the Cybersecurity graduate program, where his research and teaching focus on advanced steganography/data hiding methods and the latest active cyber defense methods and techniques. Chet is also an adjunct professor at Champlain

College, where his research and teaching focus on applying Python and other scripting languages to solve challenging problems in digital investigation and forensics.

Chet resides in the Grand Strand area of South Carolina with his wife Janet, son Matthew, two Labrador Retrievers (Bailey and Vinny), and feline tenants Lucy, Rosie, and Evander.

About the Technical Reviewer

**Gary C. Kessler**, PhD, CCE, CISSP, is a Professor of Cybersecurity and Chair of the Security Studies & International Affairs Department at Embry-Riddle Aeronautical University in Daytona Beach, Florida. His academic background is in mathematics and computer science, and his research interests include network protocols, digital forensics, and cybersecurity management and policy, particularly related to maritime and aviation. Gary is also an adjunct professor at Edith Cowan University (Perth, WA) and American Marine University (Sarasota, FL).

Gary started the undergraduate and graduate digital forensics programs at Champlain College (Burlington, VT) and has been affiliated with the National Internet Crimes Against Children (ICAC) program and Vermont, Northern Florida, and Hawaii Task Forces since 1999. He is also a frequent speaker at national and international conferences, notably the annual National Cyber Crime Conference.

Gary is also a member of the advisory board of the Maritime and Port Security Information Sharing & Analysis Organization (MPS_ISAO), holds a USCG master merchant mariner certificate, and is a Master SCUBA Diver Trainer. More information about Gary can be found at `www.garykessler.net`.

Acknowledgments

I'm deeply appreciative of Joe Giordano, the driving force behind cybersecurity research and development, and ultimately education for the past four decades. Your quiet, humble, and persistent work has and is making a true impact on the security of our nation.

I want to thank Scott vonFischer, Tony Ombrellaro, and Dave Bang for providing the catalyst for this book. Your forward thinking, ensuring that your teams learn and apply the latest scripting environments to solve challenging problems in forensics and incident response, has been a true inspiration.

To my students at Utica and Champlain colleges, who constantly surprise, challenge, and inspire me to find new ways to share my decades of experience in software and scripting development to tackle the challenges of cybercrime investigation.

To Dr. Gary Kessler for his tireless validation of my scripts and writing. He always delivers sound advice on how to make both better.

To the whole team at Apress, especially Rita Fernando and Laura Berendson, for your constant encouragement, dedication, and patience throughout this project.

To my wonderful wife Janet, who always provides me with insights and a point of view about a challenge that I never thought of. These insights often, if not always, lead to new solutions and approaches that constantly improve my work.

Introduction

The endeavor to integrate PowerShell and Python came about a couple of years ago. I was providing training for a large utility and began by teaching the members of the secure operations center, or SOC, on how to apply Python scripts during investigations and incident response. A few months later, they asked for similar training – this time using PowerShell as the scripting engine for the SOC team. Based on this, I quickly realized that PowerShell was perfect for acquisition of information across the enterprise, and Python was good at performing analysis of data that had been acquired by other tools.

Now, of course, PowerShell advocates will say that PowerShell scripts can be developed to perform detailed analysis. Likewise, Python advocates will say Python scripts can be developed to perform very capable evidence acquisition. I agree with both advocates – but only to a point. The real question is… if we combine the best of both environments, does $1 + 1 = 2$ or does $1 + 1 = 11$? I believe that the answer falls somewhere in the middle.

Thus, the purpose of the book along with the research and experimentation that went into it was to build a model, in fact two models, to integrate and leverage the best capabilities of Python and PowerShell and apply the result to digital investigation. It is important to note that this is a work in progress. I believe that the continued development of advanced PowerShell and Python capabilities that leverage the models provided here has great potential and should be pursued.

Therefore, I encourage you to experiment with the models that I have presented here and use them to develop new solutions that are desperately needed to acquire and analyze evidence collected before, during, and after a cyber incident, a cyber breach, as well as physical or cybercrimes. I also encourage you to share your work and innovations with others in our field to benefit those that fight cybercrime every day.

CHAPTER 1

An Introduction to PowerShell for Investigators

PowerShell provides a great acquistion engine for obtaining a vast array of information from live systems, servers, peripherals, mobile devices, and data-driven applications like Active Directory.

Because of Microsoft's decision to open PowerShell and provide the ability to acquire information from other non-Microsoft platforms such as Mac and Linux, the breadth of information that can be accessed is virtually limitless (with the proper credentials). Combine that with a plethora of built-in and third-party CmdLets (pronounced "command let") that can be filtered, sorted, and piped together, and you have the ultimate acquistion engine.

By adding a bridge from PowerShell to Python, we can now leverage the rich logical machine learning and deep analysis of the raw information acquired by PowerShell. Figure 1-1 depicts the core components that we will integrate in this book. The result will be a workbench for developing new innovative approaches to live investigations and incident response applications.

© Chet Hosmer 2019

C. Hosmer, *PowerShell and Python Together*, https://doi.org/10.1007/978-1-4842-4504-0_1

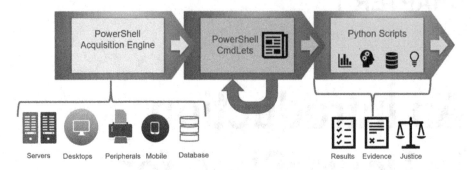

Figure 1-1. *PowerShell and Python*

A Little PowerShell History

PowerShell is a Microsoft framework that includes a command shell and a scripting language. PowerShell has traditionally been used by system administrators, IT teams, incident response groups, and forensic investigators to gain access to operational information regarding the infrastructures they manage. Signifcant evolution has occurred over the past decade as depicted in Figure 1-2.

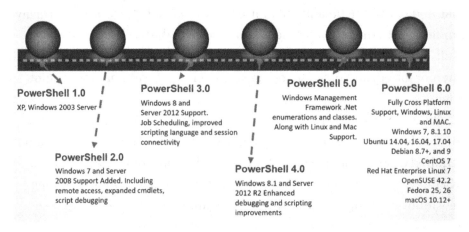

Figure 1-2. *PowerShell evolution*

How Is PowerShell Used Today?

PowerShell is most typically used to automate administrative tasks and examine the details of running desktops, servers, and mobile devices. It is used to examine both local and remote systems using the Common-Object-Model (COM) and the Windows Management Interface (WMI). Today, it can be used to examine and manage remote Linux, Mac, and Network devices using the Common Information Model (CIM).

How Do You Experiment with PowerShell?

PowerShell is typically already installed on modern Windows desktop and server platforms. If not, you can simply open your favorite browser and search for "Windows Management Framework 5" and then download and install PowerShell. PowerShell and PowerShell ISE (the Integrated Scripting Environment) are free.

I prefer using PowerShell ISE as it provides:

1. An integrated environment that aids in the discovery and experimentation with CmdLets

2. The ability to write, test, and debug scripts

3. Easy access to context-sensitive help

4. Automatic completion of commands that speed both the development and learning

Navigating PowerShell ISE

Once you have PowerShell ISE installed, you can launch it on a Windows Platform by clicking the Start Menu (bottom left corner for Windows 8-10) and then search for PowerShell ISE and click the App as shown in Figure 1-3.

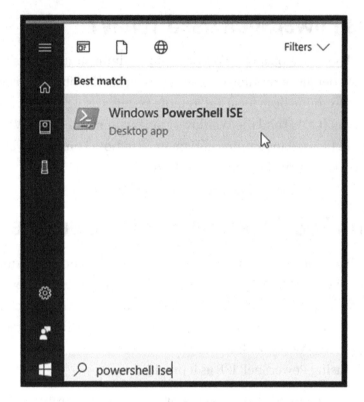

Figure 1-3. *Launching PowerShell on Windows 10*

Note   You can run PowerShell and PowerShell ISE with **User** privledge; however, to gain access to many of the rich acquisition functions needed, running PowerShell as **Administrator** is required. A word of caution as well. Running as Adminstrator or User and executing CmdLets can damage your system or delete important files! Proceed with caution!

I typically add this to my Windows Taskbar for easy access as shown in Figure 1-4. I have added both PowerShell and PowerShell ISE. The icon on the right in the highlighted box is ISE, and the one on the left is PowerShell.

By right-clicking the PowerShell ISE icon, then right-clicking again on the Windows PowerShell ISE selection you can choose to run PowerShell ISE as administrator. By doing so, you will have the ability to execute the widest range of PowerShell CmdLets and scripts.

Figure 1-4. *Windows taskbar launching PowerShell ISE as administrator*

Once launched, ISE has three main windows as shown in Figure 1-5. Note that the scripting pane is not displayed by default but can be selected for view from the toolbar. I have annotated the three main sections of the application:

1. Scripting Panel: This panel provides the ability to create PowerShell Scripts that incorporate multiple commands using the included PowerShell scripting language. Note that this is not where we typically start when developing PowerShell Scripts. Rather, we experiment in the Direct Command Entry Panel first; then once we have perfected our approach, we can then create scripts.

2. Direct Command Entry Panel: This panel is used to execute PowerShell CmdLets. The commands entered here are much more powerful than the ancestor Windows Command Line or DOS commands. In addition, the format and structure

5

of these commands is much different and follows
some strict rules. I will be explaining the verb–noun
format and structure and providing more details
and some examples in the next section.

3. Command Help Panel: This panel provides detailed
help and information regarding every CmdLet
available to us. However, I rarely use this area and
instead request direct help using the Get-Help
CmdLet to get information regarding CmdLets of
interest, to learn how they operate, get examples of
their use, and get details of all the options that are
available.

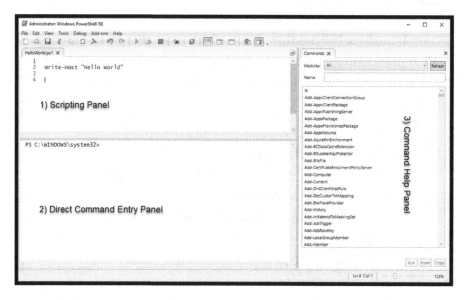

Figure 1-5. *PowerShell ISE interface*

PowerShell CmdLets

Before we dive directly into entering PowerShell CmdLets, a few words of warning:

1. There are literally thousands of possible CmdLets.

2. There are hundreds of thousands of possible options if you consider all the possible variations.

3. There are new CmdLets, variations, and updates to existing CmdLets being created every day.

4. Each CmdLet contains detailed help and examples.

It is important to update CmdLet Help every day to ensure you have access to the latest information regarding CmdLets that you are using or plan to use.

What Is a CmdLet?

A CmdLet is typically a lightweight Windows PowerShell script that performs a specific function. The reason I state typically here is that some CmdLets are quite extensive, and with the ability to create your own CmdLet, their complexity and use of system resources can vary based on the developer's objective.

A CmdLet then is a specific order from a user to the operating system, or to an application to perform a service, such as "display all the currently running processes" or "show me all the services that are currently stopped."

All CmdLets are expressed as a **verb–noun** pair and have a help file that can be accessed using the verb–noun pair `Get-Help <CmdLet name>`. So yes, even help is just another CmdLet. Updating help is vital to keep help associated with current all the currently installed CmdLets and to install help for new CmdLets that are created and updated every day.

As you might guess, this is just another CmdLet and this is the first CmdLet you should use. Specifically:

```
Update-Help
```

You can execute this CmdLet from the Direct Command Entry Panel as shown in Figure 1-6. The help files will be updated for all installed modules. We will discuss modules in a future chapter, but for now this will update all the standard PowerShell modules. Additional modules such as Active Directory, VMWare, SharePoint, and hundreds of others allow acquisition to numerous devices and services.

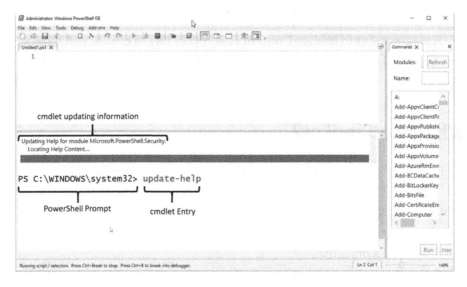

Figure 1-6. *Update-Help CmdLet execution*

Introduction to Some Key CmdLets

One of the first questions you might ask is, "What CmdLets are available?" Or more specifically, "What CmdLets are available targeting specific information?" This section will introduce you to a few key CmdLets:

Get-Help, Get-Process, and Get-Member.

Get-Help

Let's say we are interested in getting information about currently running services. In order to find the CmdLets that relate to this topic I would enter:

```
Get-Help services
```

Note that I did not request information about a specific CmdLet, rather I asked the help system to provide me with information regarding any CmdLet that could relate to services. Figure 1-7 displays an abbreviated output.

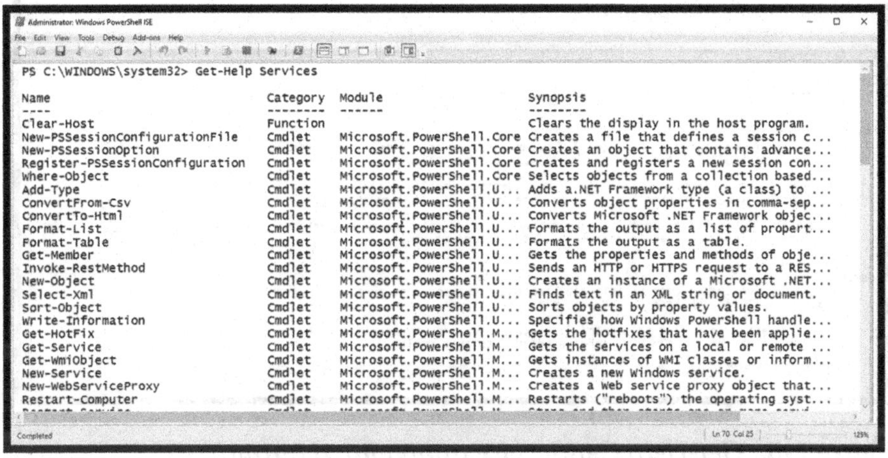

Figure 1-7. *Search for CmdLets related to services*

Note that depending on what version of PowerShell you are working with, the current version of the help file, and what CmdLets are installed, your list may differ.

The next step is to select one or more CmdLets and Get-Help for those CmdLets. Looking through the abbreviated list, Get-Service sounds promising, so I will request help on that specific CmdLet by typing:

```
Get-Help Get-Service
```

Figure 1-8 displays the abbreviated output. Note that there are multiple options related to the execution of the Get-Help CmdLet. For this example, I used the simplest form. However, optionally I could have used other forms of the CmdLet such as:

```
Get-Help Get-Service -Detailed
```

or

```
Get-Help Get-Service -Examples
```

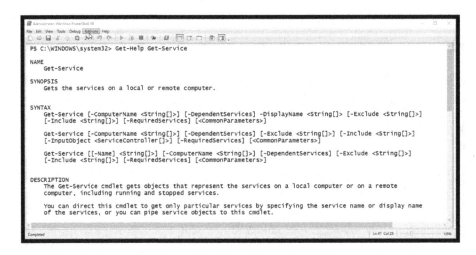

Figure 1-8. *Get-Help Get-Service abbreviated output*

Examining the output, we notice the detailed syntax presented to us for each command. This CmdLet allows us to obtain information regarding services on a local or remote computer. The option -ComputerName allows us to specify more than one computer, each separated by a comma. By using:

```
Get-Help Get-Service -Examples
```

the help system will provide numerous examples demonstrating the use of the CmdLet (Figure 1-9).

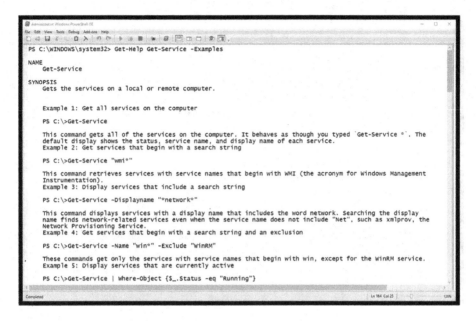

```
PS C:\WINDOWS\system32> Get-Help Get-Service -Examples

NAME
    Get-Service

SYNOPSIS
    Gets the services on a local or remote computer.


    Example 1: Get all services on the computer

    PS C:\>Get-Service

    This command gets all of the services on the computer. It behaves as though you typed `Get-Service *`. The
    default display shows the status, service name, and display name of each service.
    Example 2: Get services that begin with a search string

    PS C:\>Get-Service "wmi*"

    This command retrieves services with service names that begin with WMI (the acronym for Windows Management
    Instrumentation).
    Example 3: Display services that include a search string

    PS C:\>Get-Service -Displayname "*network*"

    This command displays services with a display name that includes the word network. Searching the display
    name finds network-related services even when the service name does not include "Net", such as xmlprov, the
    Network Provisioning Service.
    Example 4: Get services that begin with a search string and an exclusion

    PS C:\>Get-Service -Name "win*" -Exclude "WinRM"

    These commands get only the services with service names that begin with win, except for the WinRM service.
    Example 5: Display services that are currently active

    PS C:\>Get-Service | Where-Object {$_.Status -eq "Running"}
```

Figure 1-9. *Get-Help with examples*

Get-Process

Another useful CmdLet is Get-Process; much like Get-Service it returns
information regarding processes running on a local or remote computer.
Taking a deeper look at Get-Process using Get-Help (see Figure 1-10), we
first notice six different fundamental variants of Get-Process. Technically
these are called parameter sets, which allow us to run the Get-Process
CmdLet six separate ways.

```
Administrator: Windows PowerShell ISE                                              –  □  X
File  Edit  View  Tools  Debug  Add-ons  Help
PS C:\WINDOWS\system32> Get-Help Get-Process

NAME
    Get-Process

SYNOPSIS
    Gets the processes that are running on the local computer or a remote computer.

SYNTAX
    Get-Process [[-Name] <String[]>] [-ComputerName <String[]>] [-FileVersionInfo] [-Module]
    [<CommonParameters>]

    Get-Process [-ComputerName <String[]>] [-FileVersionInfo] -Id <Int32[]>] [-Module] [<CommonParameters>]

    Get-Process [-ComputerName <String[]>] [-FileVersionInfo] -InputObject <Process[]> [-Module]
    [<CommonParameters>]

    Get-Process -Id <Int32[]> -IncludeUserName [<CommonParameters>]

    Get-Process [[-Name] <String[]>] -IncludeUserName [<CommonParameters>]

    Get-Process -IncludeUserName -InputObject <Process[]> [<CommonParameters>]


DESCRIPTION
    The Get-Process cmdlet gets the processes on a local or remote computer.

    Without parameters, this cmdlet gets all of the processes on the local computer. You can also specify a
    particular process by process name or process ID (PID) or pass a process object through the pipeline to
    this cmdlet.

    By default, this cmdlet returns a process object that has detailed information about the process and
    supports methods that let you start and stop the process. You can also use the parameters of the
    Get-Process cmdlet to get file version information for the program that runs in the process and to get the
    modules that the process loaded.

Completed                                                              Ln 55 Col 25          125%
```

Figure 1-10. *Get-Help Get-Process*

Examining the first parameter set (see Figure 1-11), we find that all the parameters are optional. This is signified by the square brackets that surround each parameter.

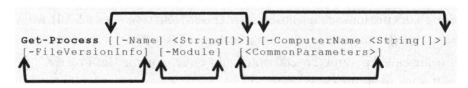

Figure 1-11. *Get-Process*

This allows us to simply type the command without including any additional parameters as shown in Figure 1-12 with abbreviated output.

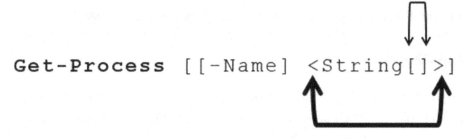

```
PS C:\WINDOWS\system32> Get-Process

Handles  NPM(K)    PM(K)    WS(K)    CPU(s)      Id  SI ProcessName
-------  ------    -----    -----    ------      --  -- -----------
    470      22     6560     4420  3,150.89   55708   2 AdobeCollabSync
    277      14     2692      748      0.23   56592   2 AdobeCollabSync
    238      23     9184     2712      0.23  113824   2 ApplePhotoStreams
    476      28    22652    24240     17.42   79164   2 ApplicationFrameHost
    157       8     1780      140      0.02  229160   0 AppVShNotify
    166       9     1952       88      0.06  254356   2 AppVShNotify
    375      25     5304     3316      2.61   17736   2 APSDaemon
    323      16     2928     1496      0.22    4240   0 armsvc
   2436      27    37908    35560    947.89    4084   0 avgsvca
   1137      39    96516    47184    882.81    2304   2 avguix
    870      26     2560     2096     29.59     608   0 csrss
   1039      23     3236     2836  1,934.00  221540   2 csrss
    556      17   173592    14056    252.80   14372   2 ctfmon
    541      19     9904     8708    241.78    2756   0 dasHost
    143      10     2608      896      0.03  183140   0 DbxSvc
   2207      38    44976    25248     89.72    8352   0 DellSupportAssistRemedationService
    192      16     3096     2936      0.33   62820   0 dllhost
    331      16     5348     4336      1.73  117980   2 dllhost
    229      19     4716      536      0.48  145176   2 dllhost
    330      16     5532    14384     12.84  174392   2 dllhost
    150       9     1404       88      0.02   98492   2 Dropbox
    172      12     1940     1164      0.47  112280   2 Dropbox
   8567     169   248656   152988  4,867.97  132676   2 Dropbox
    214      14     2480      124      8.66    7836   0 DropboxUpdate
   1259      56   145856   115792 16,312.86  219448   2 dwm
   1668      83   174940   128020     44.83  252540   2 EXCEL
  12736     434   317284   207280  4,862.30    4424   2 explorer
     44       6     2016      324      0.48     396   0 fontdrvhost
     44      11     7560     6392     41.41  221500   2 fontdrvhost
    984      41    39280    18828  2,563.80   20388   2 g2mcomm
    744      33    19872     7716     12.81    3524   2 g2mlauncher
    424      19     6016     1536      0.59   22324   2 g2mstart
```

Figure 1-12. *Get-Process with no additional parameters*

What if I would like to obtain information only related to the process associated with the Google Chrome browser? In Figure 1-13, I break out the specific -Name Parameter that we need to utilize in order to accomplish this.

```
Get-Process  [[-Name]  <String[]>]
```

Figure 1-13. *Get-Process -Name parameter*

You notice that the -Name Parameter is optional; however, if it is specified, you must specify a String indicating the specific type of data you must provide (the content of which would be the name of the process). You also notice that following the word String there are two square brackets. This indicates that you can optionally include a list of names. Each name needs to be separated by a comma. Figure 1-14 shows an example.

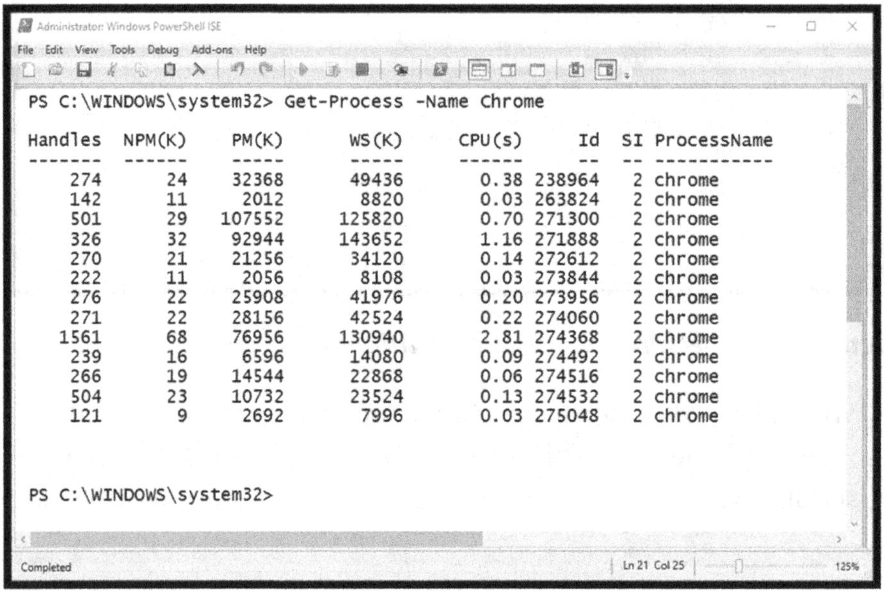

Figure 1-14. Get-Process example using -Name parameter

Get-Member

As you have seen, PowerShell CmdLets provide useful results when using them to obtain information (or evidence) from a target system. In addition to the simple output, each CmdLet also returns an object that provides access to additional properties and methods. The Get-Member CmdLet will display the available properties and methods for a CmdLet.

Note that as with any CmdLet, you can utilize the Get-Help CmdLet to obtain details and examples regarding Get-Member. For example, the command would be:

```
Get-Help Get-Member
```

To illustrate the value of obtaining additional properties of a CmdLet, look at the standard output of the Get-Service CmdLet as shown in Figure 1-15.

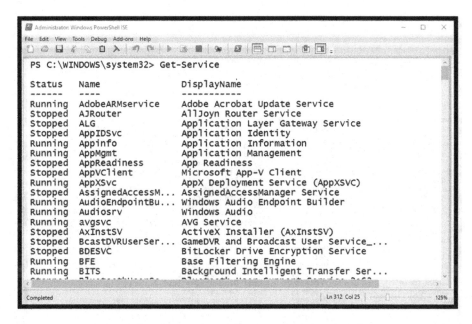

Figure 1-15. *Standard output of the Get-Service CmdLet*

What if additional information evidence is required? For example, what if it was important to know how the service was started? In order to answer this question, we need to interrogate and obtain additional properties from the object.

To extract the method and property details of an object, we need to utilize a pipe to direct the output object to the Get-Member CmdLet. Pipes operate similarly in most command line and shell environments. However, in PowerShell they are object and context specific.

The CmdLet that we wish to interrogate in this example, Get-Service, is not executed, but rather the object information is passed to the Get-Member CmdLet as shown in Figure 1-16. Note the name of the property we are looking for is StartType.

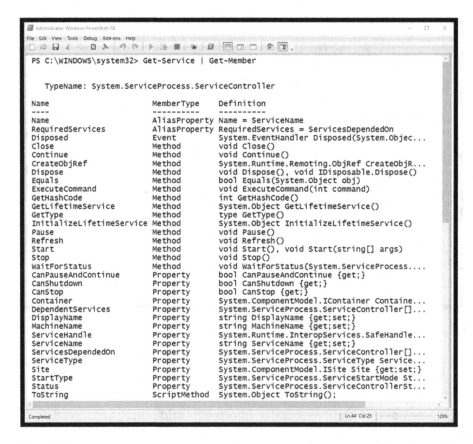

Figure 1-16. *Get-Member example*

Now that we know the name, we can specify that property StartType displays a customized output as shown in Figure 1-17. This is the simplest form of piping we can perform. The Get-Service CmdLet is executed, and the results are piped to the Select-Object CmdLet.

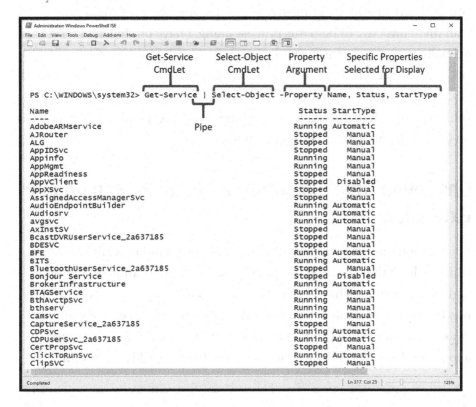

Figure 1-17. *Get-Service with name, status, and StartType*

The Select-Object CmdLet then displays the specific properties specified. The -Property argument of the Select-Object CmdLet accepts string names that are to be displayed. Again, each is separated by a comma.

Challenge Problems: Investigative CmdLets to Explore

To become comfortable with PowerShell, the ISE, and the CmdLets that you are likely to utilize during investigations, you need to experiment with them directly. To help this process along, I have put together a set of challenge problems at the end of each chapter. Remember to use Get-Help with each of the CmdLets, and make sure you use -Detailed and -Examples options when examining the CmdLets. I have also provided solutions to each of the challenge problems in the Appendix, so try these on your own and then check your results.

Challenge One: Executing a "Find" Based on File Extension

Many of you may be familiar with Windows Command Line dir command, which will list the contents of a specific directory. All traditional Windows and DOS commands have equivalent PowerShell commands. An effortless way to find the equivalent is to **use** a PowerShell CmdLet to find the associated PowerShell CmdLet as shown in Figure 1-18. To learn more about Get-Alias and Get-ChildItem, use the PowerShell Help system.

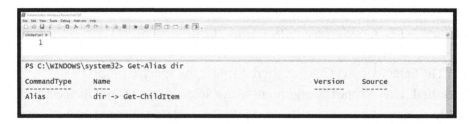

Figure 1-18. *Using Get-Alias*

Now that you know about the Get-ChildItem CmdLet, use this to find all files on your system with the .jpg extension.

Feel free to experiment with other parameters provided with Get-ChildItem. Also, make sure you access Get-Help using the -Examples switch and study those examples.

Challenge Two: Examining Network Settings

At this point you might be thinking, "If PowerShell simply replaces Windows Command Line, then why not just use the Windows Command Line?" As was learned earlier in this chapter, the help system can provide a list of available commands surrounding a specific word or phrase.

Try typing:

```
Get-Help ip
```

This will provide all PowerShell CmdLets that involve IP. You will see a number of possible CmdLets that allow you to examine your network configuration. Notice that this is much more powerful than using Windows Command Line. For this challenge, take a deep look at just three of these CmdLets:

```
Get-NetIPAddress
Get-NetIPConfiguration
Get-NetIPInterface
```

Start by using the PowerShell help system to understand the capabilities of each CmdLet and examine the examples provided. Then experiment with each of the commands and take a close look at your own network settings. Were you aware of all the settings?

Challenge Three: Examining Firewall Settings

For this challenge problem, find possible firewall related CmdLets. Specifically get information regarding the firewall settings on your system. Once you have examined the basic information find and execute a CmdLet that will examine any "Service Filters" that are enabled. Did you discover any surprises?

Challenge Four: Your Chance to Explore

For this challenge, use the help system and keywords that you would be interested in probing your system for.

Summary

This chapter introduced the goals of this book, specifically how the integration of PowerShell and Python would provide value to investigators.

In addition, a brief evolution of PowerShell was covered to better understand how PowerShell today is relevant to investigations. The basic setup and execution of PowerShell and where to obtain the latest trusted version were provided. An overview of PowerShell ISE and the PowerShell help system was provided along with the importance of updating the help system. Next, PowerShell CmdLets and the verb–noun vernacular were introduced followed by a brief discussion and examples of how to identify specific CmdLets of interest. Several CmdLets were demonstrated to provide details regarding the depth of information that can be acquired with PowerShell. Finally, a set of challenge problems were presented to encourage you to dive in and experiment with PowerShell.

Looking forward to Chapter 2, we'll find that one of the key elements of PowerShell CmdLets is the ability to create PowerShell variables and string together multiple commands in a method called Pipelining. We will establish several investigative challenges and solve them with PowerShell variables and Pipelining. In addition, we will introduce several new CmdLets that will allow us to sort, filter, and format the output. Chapter 2 is key as it provides a prelude to how we will be integrating PowerShell with Python.

CHAPTER 2

PowerShell Pipelining

Pipelining is the key feature within PowerShell that will help us facilitate the integration of Python and PowerShell. The examples and illustrations in this chapter were chosen to explain pipelining and provide insight into CmdLet and methods that are useful during investigations.

What Is CmdLet Pipelining?

CmdLet Pipelining creates an assembly line of commands to be executed in a specific sequence while moving the data or results from each CmdLet as well. The best way to describe this is with a couple of investigation-related examples.

Example 1: Get-Service

Assume that we want to see what services are currently **running** on a system we are investigating. The filtering down of the output from one CmdLet to another is one of the most common uses of the pipeline. In addition, we would like to display the output in a table format. Figure 2-1 is a sample pipeline that will solve this challenge.

© Chet Hosmer 2019
C. Hosmer, *PowerShell and Python Together*, https://doi.org/10.1007/978-1-4842-4504-0_2

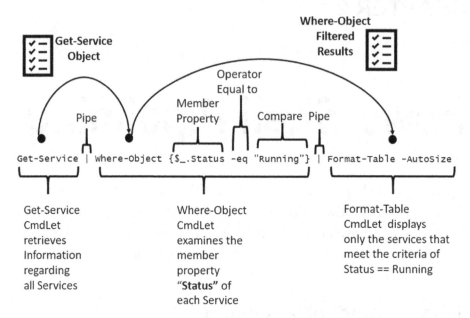

Figure 2-1. *Pipeline illustration for display of running services*

As you can see, the pipeline starts with the Get-Service CmdLet without any command line parameters.

Note   You could of course add command line parameters before the pipe symbol I such as -ComputerName which would allow the Get-Service CmdLet to execute a remotely on the specified computer.

The Get-Service CmdLet produces an object that is passed across the Pipeline to the next Cmdlet in the chain.

The Where-Object CmdLet performs a filtering action that evaluates the Get-Service CmdLet Object Property **Status** equal to "Running." The resulting output of the Where-Object CmdLet filters the results to only include those services that are currently running. The result is then passed to the next Pipeline CmdLet.

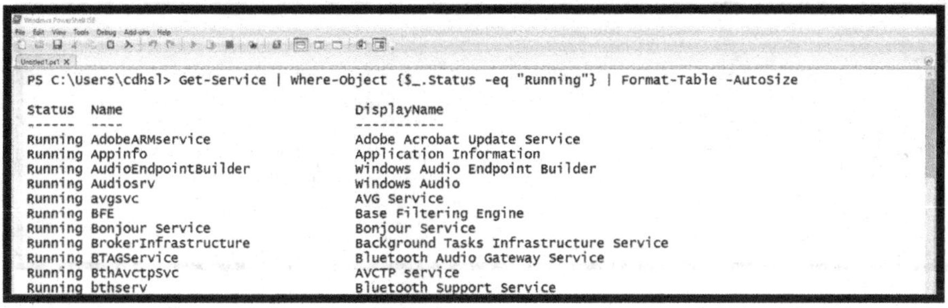

```
PS C:\Users\cdhsl> Get-Service | Where-Object {$_.Status -eq "Running"} | Format-Table -AutoSize

Status  Name                         DisplayName
------  ----                         -----------
Running AdobeARMservice              Adobe Acrobat Update Service
Running Appinfo                      Application Information
Running AudioEndpointBuilder         Windows Audio Endpoint Builder
Running Audiosrv                     Windows Audio
Running avgsvc                       AVG Service
Running BFE                          Base Filtering Engine
Running Bonjour Service              Bonjour Service
Running BrokerInfrastructure         Background Tasks Infrastructure Service
Running BTAGService                  Bluetooth Audio Gateway Service
Running BthAvctpSvc                  AVCTP service
Running bthserv                      Bluetooth Support Service
```

Figure 2-2. *Challenge solution*

Finally, Format-Table CmdLet produces a table result display with the filter services using the default output associated with Get-Service. Figure 2-2 depicts the actual command in action – the results were truncated for brevity.

Note By using the Get-Service | Get-Member operation, you can reveal all the methods and properties available within the Get-Service CmdLet object allowing for additional filtering options.

Reporting which services are stopped can be equally important during an investigation. For example, sophisticated malicious software will disable virus protection, firewalls, and other defensive services designed for protection. Figure 2-3 changes the command to display only the services that are currently stopped. Again, the results were truncated for brevity.

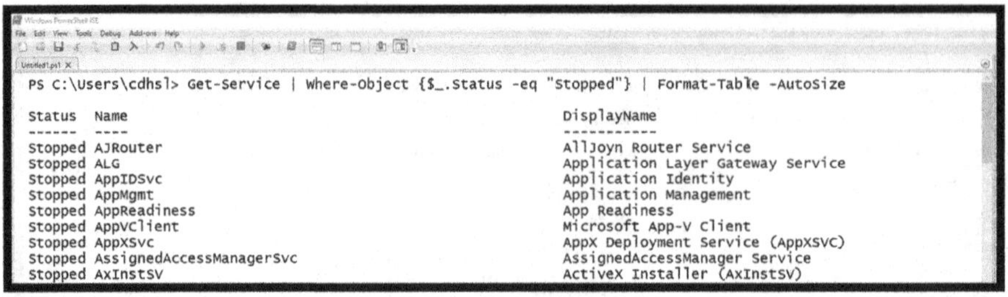

Figure 2-3. *Displaying stopped services*

One final note: If you want more information regarding Format-Table, remember to use Get-Help as shown in Figure 2-4.

Figure 2-4. *Format-Table CmdLet overview*

Example 2: Get-Process

Details related to running processes are also important and can provide additional information regarding what processes are connected to. For example, it might be important in a live investigation to determine what active Internet connections are in use by Google Chrome. For this example, let's first break this down into the individual components and introduce the concept of variables in PowerShell.

PowerShell Variables

What are PowerShell variables: A variable in PowerShell is simply a named place in memory assigned to hold data values. All variable names in PowerShell begin with a **$** making them easy to identify. One additional note: Variable names in PowerShell are NOT case sensitive; thus, $ipAddress and $IPaddress represent the same variable. You can assign values to variables such as:

```
$InvestigatorName = "Chet Hosmer"
```

or

```
$CaseNumber = "BC-0234"
```

PowerShell Automatic Variables

In addition, there are several built-in or automatic variables that are available but cannot be changed by the user. Several examples are shown in Figure 2-5.

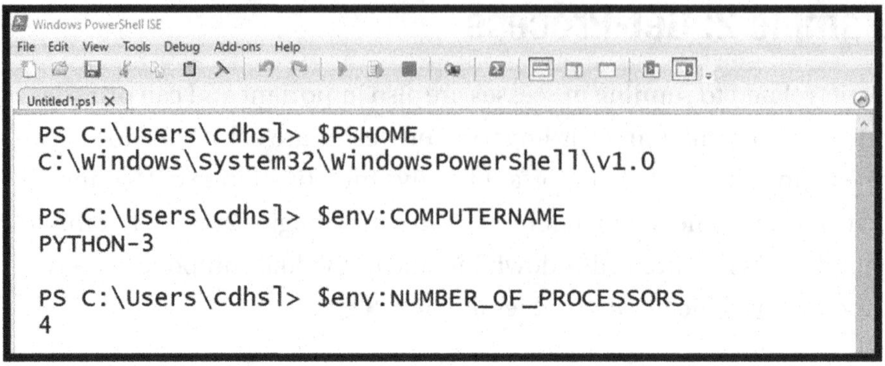

```
Windows PowerShell ISE
File  Edit  View  Tools  Debug  Add-ons  Help

Untitled1.ps1 X

PS C:\Users\cdhsl> $PSHOME
c:\Windows\System32\WindowsPowerShell\v1.0

PS C:\Users\cdhsl> $env:COMPUTERNAME
PYTHON-3

PS C:\Users\cdhsl> $env:NUMBER_OF_PROCESSORS
4
```

Figure 2-5. Example of automatic variables

Breaking Down the CmdLet Usage for Example 2

Now that we have a general idea about variables, we will put them to use in gather information from Get-Process. In order to reduce the output from Get-Process, let's focus on just one running process. On my test system I have Google Chrome installed and running. On your system you may be using other browsers such as Internet Explorer or Firefox. Substitute the name of your browser to target the processes that are created by them. Also, the process named svchost is always running, therefore you can substitute that as well. The command within PowerShell to do this is as follows, and the results are shown in Figure 2-6.

```
Get-Process -Name chrome
```

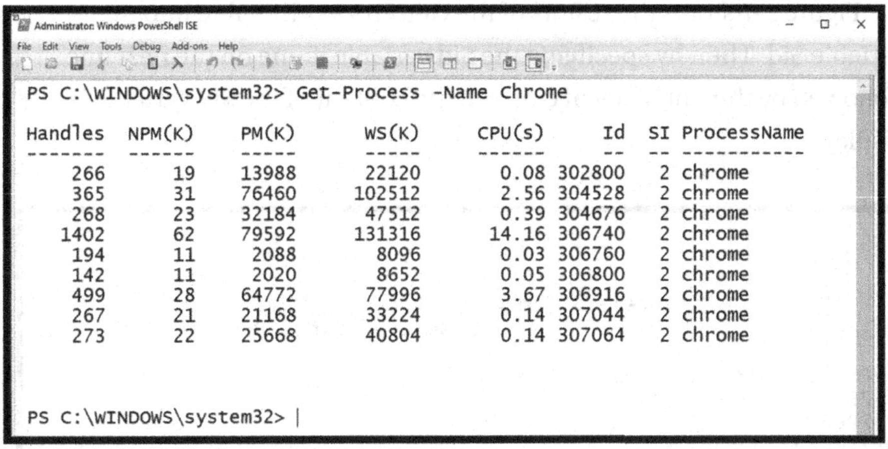

Figure 2-6. *Get-Process -Name Chrome*

A key piece of information that is needed from the Get-Process CmdLet is the Process ID associated in my example with Google Chrome. We can use this Process ID to correlate the process with associated Internet activity. As you probably guessed we will be using yet another CmdLet in PowerShell to examine the connections between Google Chrome and the Internet. In order to accomplish this, a command will be constructed to store the results of the CmdLet into a variable, named $id, instead of simply displaying the results:

```
$id = Get-Process -Name Chrome `
  | select -ExpandProperty Id
```

Notice that I used the tick (`) character and then Shift+Enter to continue the command on the next line for easy display. The results of the Get-Process -Name Chrome command are then piped to select the -ExpandProperty command to specify only the Id field. You can of course enter this command on a single line, but it is a nice way to make this more readable.

Figure 2-7 stores the results of the Get-Process ID value into the variable $id. Then by specifying the $id variable name on the next line (followed by the Enter key of course), the content of the $id variable is displayed.

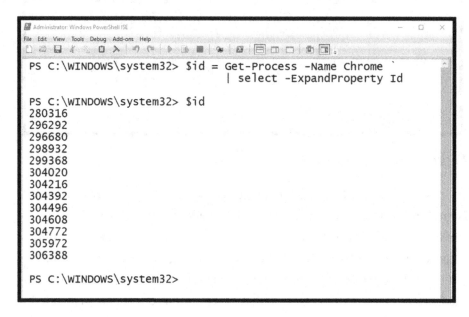

Figure 2-7. *Store the Get-Process CmdLet results in the variable $id*

Adding the NetTCPConnections CmdLet

The $id variable can now be utilized as a parameter to other CmdLets. For example, the CmdLet Get-NetTCPConnections has a parameter -OwningProcess, which allows us to restrict the output of the CmdLet to target specific Process IDs. Examining Get-NetTCPConnections using Get-Help, the following information is obtained (see Figure 2-8).

```
NAME
    Get-NetTCPConnection

SYNOPSIS
    Gets TCP connections.

SYNTAX
    Get-NetTCPConnection [[-LocalAddress] <String[]>] [[-LocalPort] <UInt16[]>]
    [-AppliedSetting <AppliedSetting[]>] [-CimSession <CimSession[]>] [-CreationTime
    <DateTime[]>] [-OffloadState <OffloadState[]>] [-OwningProcess <UInt32[]>]
    [-RemoteAddress <String[]>] [-RemotePort <UInt16[]>] [-State <State[]>] [-ThrottleLimit
    <Int32>] [<CommonParameters>]


DESCRIPTION
    The Get-NetTCPConnection cmdlet gets current TCP connections. Use this cmdlet to view
    TCP connection properties such as local or remote IP address, local or remote port, and
    connection state.
```

Figure 2-8. *Get-NetTCPConnections help*

How to Discover CmdLets?

One of the questions you might be asking is with thousands of CmdLets
how would I know which one to use to obtain and associated TCP
connections with the Owning Process? The answer is using Get-Help. The
design of the help system built into PowerShell is key to getting the most
out of PowerShell and the associated CmdLets. Since the Help system is
updated everyday it is designed to keep pace with new CmdLets that are
created along with any updates to existing CmdLets. However, you can also
find CmdLets that are related to specific keywords. For example, see how
to use Get-Help using a keyword instead of a CmdLet in Figure 2-9.

```
PS C:\Users\cdhs1> Get-Help TCP

Name                    Category  Module     Synopsis
----                    --------  ------     --------
Get-NetTCPConnection    Function  NetTCPIP   Gets TCP connections.
Get-NetTCPSetting       Function  NetTCPIP   Gets information about TCP settings and c...
Set-NetTCPSetting       Function  NetTCPIP   Modifies a TCP setting.
```

Figure 2-9. *Get-Help using a keyword instead of a CmdLet*

31

When you provide Get-Help with a keyword as in this case **TCP** it will report known CmdLets that have any association with TCP. As you can see, Get-NetTCPConnection is the first hit. Once you know the name of the CmdLet, you can then use Get-Help with the CmdLet name to determine how to use it as I did in Figure 2-8.

Using PowerShell Variables with CmdLets

Executing the Get-NetTCPConnection CmdLet using the -OwningProcess parameter and specifying $id will generate only the TCP Connections associated with the Google Chrome id values discovered earlier using Get-Process. The command to accomplish this is as follows, with an example output shown in Figure 2-10.

```
Get-NetTCPConnection -State Established -OwningProcess $id |
Format-Table -Autosize
```

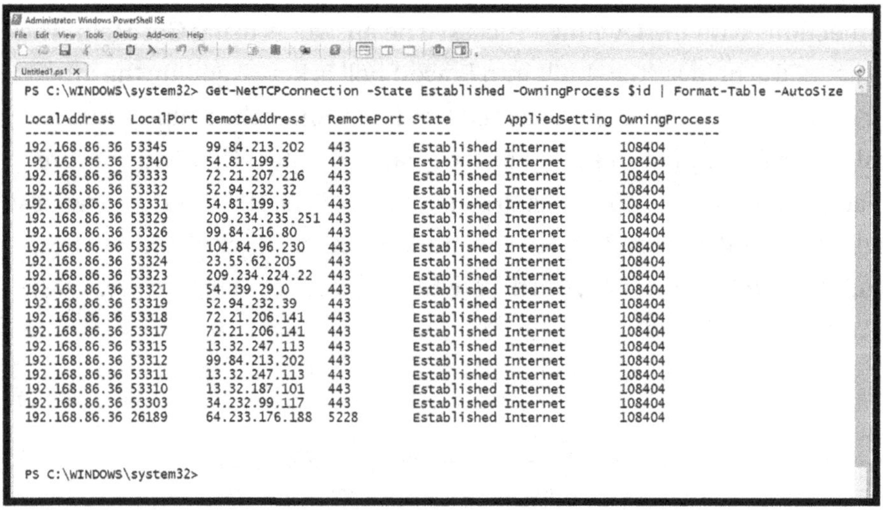

Figure 2-10. *Executing Get-NetTCPConnection with a variable for Process ID*

As you can see, the command line parameters -State and -OwningProcess are utilized:

- For -State, **Established** is specified as the argument. This will list only the TCP connections that are currently connected, as I'm only interested in current connections right now.

- For -OwningProcess, instead, the variable $id is specified, which contains a list of Process IDs associated with Google Chrome. The reason this works is that the definition provided by Get-Help for the parameter -OwningProcess is stated as follows:

```
[-OwningProcess <UInt32[]>]
```

The definition states that -OwningProcess requires an Unsigned Integer with a length of 32 bits. The two brackets [] following UInt32 indicate that it can accept a list of values.

As you can see, only one of the Chrome Process IDs (specifically, 108404) is associated with established Internet connections. Therefore, the other Google Chrome processes that were identified do not make direct Internet connections, only 108404 does.

This is a great example of how to use an intermediate variable to store the contents of a command. However, we can perform this operation using a single command. Armed with the knowledge of the workings of Get-Process, PowerShell variables, and Get-NetTCPConnections, a single command can be created that eliminates the need for the $id variable. In order to take this next step, the ForEach-Object CmdLet is needed.

ForEach-Object

ForEach-Object allows the processing of each subsequent result from the previous command on the pipeline. In this example, that would be each result generated by the Get-Process -Name Chrome command.

Figure 2-11 uses Get-Help to provide an explanation of the For-Each-Object.

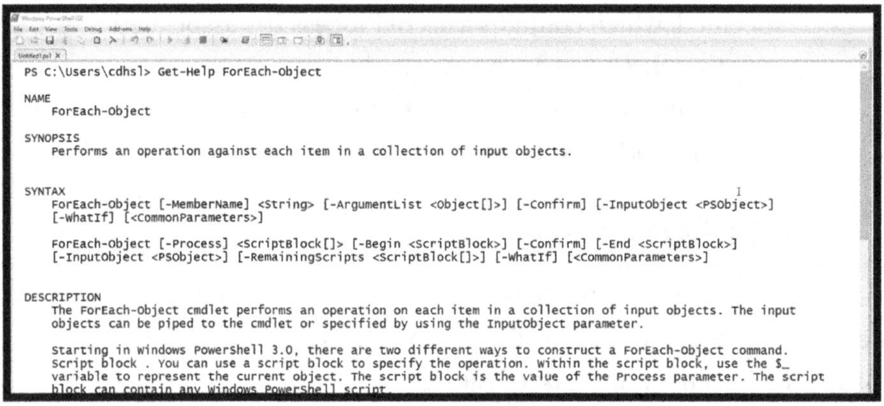

Figure 2-11. *Get-Help overview of ForEach-Object*

Creating a Single Pipeline Solution to Example 2

```
Get-Process -Name Chrome | ForEach-Object {Get-NetTCPConnection
-State Established -OwningProcess $_.Id -ErrorAction
SilentlyContinue}| Format-Table -Autosize
```

In this example (see the results of the operation in Figure 2-12), the components are broken down as follows:

```
Get-Process -Name Chrome
```

- Obtains process details for all processes named Chrome.

    ```
    ForEach-Object { }
    ```

- Processes each iteration (in simpler terms each output supplied by Get-Process via the pipe.

  ```
  {Get-NetTCPConnection -State Established
  -OwningProcess $_.Id -ErrorAction SilentlyContinue}
  ```

- Executes the Get-NetTCPConnection CmdLet for each result.

- -State Established filters the output to only include currently established connections.

- -OwningProcess $_.Id specifies the Process ID that connection information will be extracted. The $_.Id syntax is used to obtain the Process ID of the Owning Process from each iterative result of the Get-Process CmdLet. The specific property is addressed using the following syntax:

  - $_.Id

    This syntax breaks down as follows:

    - $_ represents the current object passed over the pipe.

    - .Id specifies which specific property value is associated with the operation.

- -ErrorAction -SilentlyContinue is used to ignore any errors that may occur during the Get-NetTCPConnection CmdLet. For example, if the Process ID is not linked to a specified TCPConnection the CmdLet will throw and exception. This parameter allows those exceptions to be ignored.

- Format-Table -Autosize is used to format the output in a more compact format.

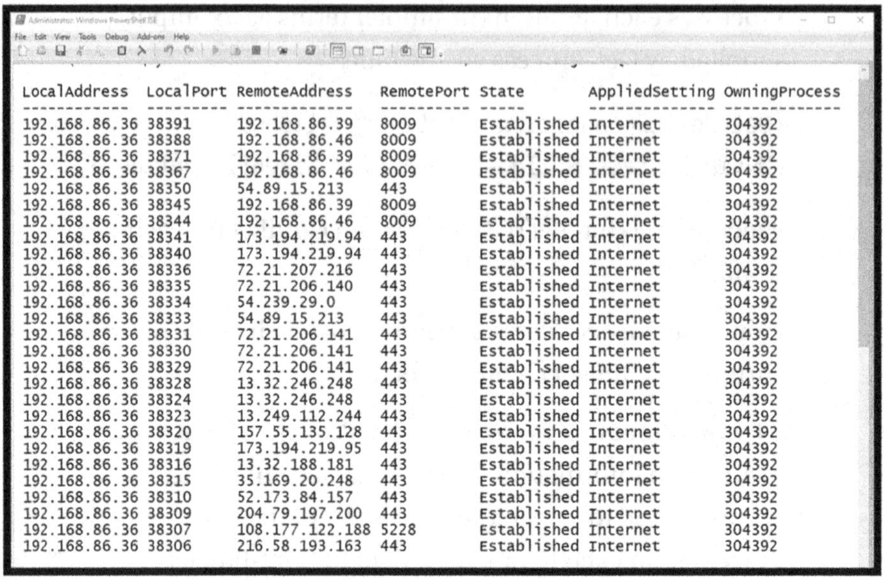

```
LocalAddress   LocalPort RemoteAddress   RemotePort State           AppliedSetting OwningProcess
------------   --------- -------------   ---------- -----           -------------- -------------
192.168.86.36  38391     192.168.86.39   8009       Established Internet        304392
192.168.86.36  38388     192.168.86.46   8009       Established Internet        304392
192.168.86.36  38371     192.168.86.39   8009       Established Internet        304392
192.168.86.36  38367     192.168.86.46   8009       Established Internet        304392
192.168.86.36  38350     54.89.15.213    443        Established Internet        304392
192.168.86.36  38345     192.168.86.39   8009       Established Internet        304392
192.168.86.36  38344     192.168.86.46   8009       Established Internet        304392
192.168.86.36  38341     173.194.219.94  443        Established Internet        304392
192.168.86.36  38340     173.194.219.94  443        Established Internet        304392
192.168.86.36  38336     72.21.207.216   443        Established Internet        304392
192.168.86.36  38335     72.21.206.140   443        Established Internet        304392
192.168.86.36  38334     54.239.29.0     443        Established Internet        304392
192.168.86.36  38333     54.89.15.213    443        Established Internet        304392
192.168.86.36  38331     72.21.206.141   443        Established Internet        304392
192.168.86.36  38330     72.21.206.141   443        Established Internet        304392
192.168.86.36  38329     72.21.206.141   443        Established Internet        304392
192.168.86.36  38328     13.32.246.248   443        Established Internet        304392
192.168.86.36  38324     13.32.246.248   443        Established Internet        304392
192.168.86.36  38323     13.249.112.244  443        Established Internet        304392
192.168.86.36  38320     157.55.135.128  443        Established Internet        304392
192.168.86.36  38319     173.194.219.95  443        Established Internet        304392
192.168.86.36  38316     13.32.188.181   443        Established Internet        304392
192.168.86.36  38315     35.169.20.248   443        Established Internet        304392
192.168.86.36  38310     52.173.84.157   443        Established Internet        304392
192.168.86.36  38309     204.79.197.200  443        Established Internet        304392
192.168.86.36  38307     108.177.122.188 5228       Established Internet        304392
192.168.86.36  38306     216.58.193.163  443        Established Internet        304392
```

Figure 2-12. *Final solution to map Google Chrome IP connections*

Resolving Remote IP Addresses

These results bring up the next investigative question, what do the IP addresses referenced by the Chrome browser refer to? There is of course a CmdLet that can discover this information directly. The IP address 72.21.207.216 was arbitrarily selected from the list in Figure 2-12. The Resolve-DnsName CmdLet was then used to obtain information regarding this remote IP address.

```
Resolve-DnsName 72.21.207.216
```

The Resolve-DnsName CmdLet successfully resolved the IP address with developer.amazonservices.com (see Figure 2-13).

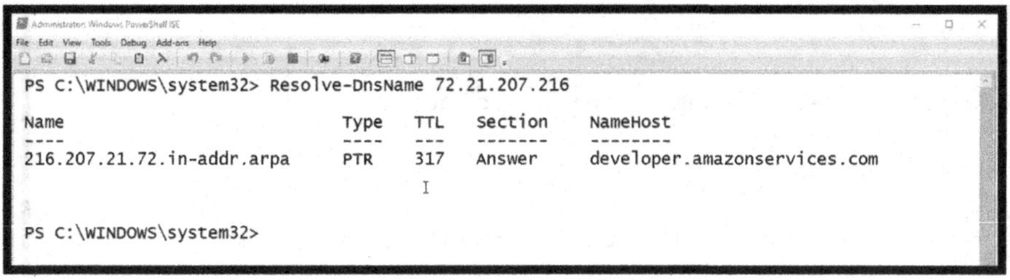

```
PS C:\WINDOWS\system32> Resolve-DnsName 72.21.207.216

Name                          Type  TTL  Section   NameHost
----                          ----  ---  -------   --------
216.207.21.72.in-addr.arpa    PTR   317  Answer    developer.amazonservices.com
                                            I

PS C:\WINDOWS\system32>
```

Figure 2-13. *Resolve DnsName*

To find out more information regarding Resolve-DnsName, try your hand at using Get-Help.

Adding a Transcript to Track Your Activities

Documentation of your investigative actions is important (to say the least). One of the simple methods of capturing your actions and the result data is to use yet another CmdLet in PowerShell:

Start-Transaction
Stop-Transaction

As with all CmdLets in PowerShell obtaining information regarding the use and options associated with CmdLets is by using Get-Help. This may sound a bit redundant; however, many people still turn to Google or other search engines to obtain this knowledge. This is certainly useful in certain circumstances, but the Help system in PowerShell is not only powerful and well thought out, but is also updated daily. Therefore, in order to get the latest, most up-to-date, and accurate information about CmdLets, use Get-Help. Figure 2-14 provides the results relating to Start-Transcript.

Figure 2-14. *Get-Help Start-Transcript*

For this example, the -Path parameter is specified in order to direct the output of the transcript to a specific file as shown in Figure 2-15. To demonstrate the -Append parameter of Start-Transcript, the Stop-Transcript CmdLet was used, and then Transcript was restarted. To accomplish this, just start the second Start-Transcript CmdLet using the same -Path parameter, and then add the -Append option as shown in Figure 2-15. This allows you to concatenate PowerShell sessions in the same output file.

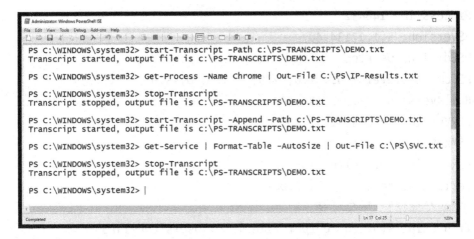

Figure 2-15. *PowerShell Start- and Stop-Transcript*

Listing 2-1 depicts the resulting transcript file. Note that yet another new CmdLet was added here, Out-File – this directs the output of the Get-Process CmdLet to the IP-Result.txt file on the desktop. Thus, the transcript does not include the Get-Process or Get-Service output, but rather that result is stored in the designated output files. This would likely be your case folder. The Start and End Time strings of each appended transaction are highlighted. Note that PowerShell uses local time; in this example, the transcript started on November 27, 2018, at 16:09:03, or 4:09 PM.

Listing 2-1. PowerShell Transcript

```
**********************
Windows PowerShell transcript start
Start time: 20181127160903
Username: PYTHON-3\cdhsl
RunAs User: PYTHON-3\cdhsl
Configuration Name:
Machine: PYTHON-3 (Microsoft Windows NT 10.0.17134.0)
Host Application: C:\WINDOWS\system32\WindowsPowerShell\v1.0\
PowerShell_ISE.exe
```

Process ID: 148432
PSVersion: 5.1.17134.407
PSEdition: Desktop
PSCompatibleVersions: 1.0, 2.0, 3.0, 4.0, 5.0, 5.1.17134.407
BuildVersion: 10.0.17134.407
CLRVersion: 4.0.30319.42000
WSManStackVersion: 3.0
PSRemotingProtocolVersion: 2.3
SerializationVersion: 1.1.0.1
****

Transcript started, output file is C:\Users\cdhsl\PS-
TRANSCRIPTS\DEMO.txt
PS C:\WINDOWS\system32> Get-Process -Name chrome | Out-File
C:\Users\cdhsl\Desktop\IP-Result.txt
PS C:\WINDOWS\system32> Stop-Transcript
****

Windows PowerShell transcript end
End time: **20181127160930**
****

****
Windows PowerShell transcript start
Start time: **20181127161013**
Username: PYTHON-3\cdhsl
RunAs User: PYTHON-3\cdhsl
Configuration Name:
Machine: PYTHON-3 (Microsoft Windows NT 10.0.17134.0)
Host Application: C:\WINDOWS\system32\WindowsPowerShell\v1.0\
PowerShell_ISE.exe
Process ID: 148432
PSVersion: 5.1.17134.407
PSEdition: Desktop

```
PSCompatibleVersions: 1.0, 2.0, 3.0, 4.0, 5.0, 5.1.17134.407
BuildVersion: 10.0.17134.407
CLRVersion: 4.0.30319.42000
WSManStackVersion: 3.0
PSRemotingProtocolVersion: 2.3
SerializationVersion: 1.1.0.1
**********************
Transcript started, output file is C:\Users\cdhsl\PS-
TRANSCRIPTS\DEMO.txt
PS C:\WINDOWS\system32> Get-Service | Format-Table -AutoSize |
Out-File C:\Users\cdhsl\Desktop\Services.txt
PS C:\WINDOWS\system32> Stop-Transcript
**********************
Windows PowerShell transcript end
End time: 20181127161306
**********************
```

Challenge Problem: CmdLet Experimentation

Working with PowerShell cannot be learned by simply reading this text or any other for that matter. Instead, you must experience PowerShell by interacting with it. Table 2-1 provides a short list of some popular CmdLets that are useful during an investigation. I have only chosen CmdLets that retrieve or acquire information for you to experiment with.

Table 2-1. *Challenge Problem CmdLets*

Get-Process	Get-Service
Get-NetIPAddress	Get-NetIPConfiguration
Get-NetIPv4Protocol	Get-NetIPv6Protocol
Get-NetTCPConnection	Test-NetConnection
Get-NetRoute	Get-MpComputerStatus
Get-MpThreat	Get-NetFirewallSetting
Get-NetFirewallPortFilter	Get-Volume
Get-ChildItem	Get-ItemProperty
Get-EventLog	Get-LocalUser
Get-LocalGroup	Get-Content
Get-Location	Set-Location
Start-Transcript	Stop-Transcript
Format-Table	

Warning   If you decide to experiment with other CmdLets that modify the system, do so at your own risk. PowerShell CmdLets can modify, damage, delete, and even destroy your system.

For each of the CmdLets specified in Table 2-1, do the following:

1. Review the help for each CmdLet including Details and Examples, that is,

    a. Get-Help -Detailed

    b. Get-Help -Examples

2. After review, describe what the CmdLet does and consider how it could be valuable during an investigation.

3. Execute each CmdLet with a minimum of one parameter, experiment with others as well.

4. Use Pipelining to assemble CmdLets, start with something simple like piping the CmdLet output to the Format-Table CmdLet, then try other options as well.

5. Make sure that your Start, and Stop the transcript during your experimentation, this will serve as a record of your actions and result. These can be referenced later when you are trying to duplicate a complex command.

Solutions to this Challenge Problem can be found in the Appendix and in the book's source code, available at www.apress.com/9781484245033.

Summary

This chapter focused on several key areas of PowerShell and introduced several new CmdLets and their application. In addition, the creation and use of PowerShell variables was introduced. Two example pipelines were created to demonstrate how to approach pipelining within PowerShell. In Chapter 3, new CmdLets will be introduced, and the development of multiple complete PowerShell scripts will be developed.

CHAPTER 3

PowerShell Scripting Targeting Investigation

This chapter will move beyond single line commands and pipelining, in order to create actual PowerShell scripts. PowerShell scripts deliver the ability to automate repetitive tasks that require specific CmdLets, Pipelines, Variables, Structures, etc. Another simple way to describe PowerShell scripts is that they allow you to create new and more powerful and targeted CmdLets to solve a specific challenge. Once you have developed a command that does exactly what you need, it is quite beneficial to create a script that encapsulates or abstracts the complexity of the command.

In this chapter, we will go through two examples. One will be to create a specific and ultimately useful investigation script that will acquire and process system event logs. The second example will be a scenario where we examine USB device usage.

© Chet Hosmer 2019
C. Hosmer, *PowerShell and Python Together*, https://doi.org/10.1007/978-1-4842-4504-0_3

Basic Facts About PowerShell Scripts

Before we begin, here are some basic facts about PowerShell scripts:

1. Scripts are a simple text file that contains a series of PowerShell commands.

2. To prevent the execution of malicious scripts, PowerShell enforces an execution policy, which by default is set to "restricted" such that PowerShell scripts will NOT execute by default. Thus, you must set the execution policy to allow script execution.

3. To execute a PowerShell script, you either must execute them within the PowerShell ISE and provide the full path to the script or the directory containing the script must be in your Windows path.

Example 1: The EventProcessor PowerShell Script

The acquisition of data from event logs is a common practice during forensic investigations and incident response activities. This is also a useful activity for system administrators to perform daily.

The collection of meaningful data from log files that are likely distributed across the investigation environment can be time consuming, and if not done consistently and completely, it will lead to problems. Therefore, developing a targeted PowerShell script to perform this operation would yield significant value to investigators.

EventLog CmdLets

Of course, PowerShell already contains general-purpose CmdLets that
address basic collection of data from event logs; thus, identifying and
selecting one of the available CmdLets is the first step. To do this we once
again turn to the built-in PowerShell Help system. Requesting Help using
the keyword EventLog returns the CmdLet list as shown in Figure 3-1.

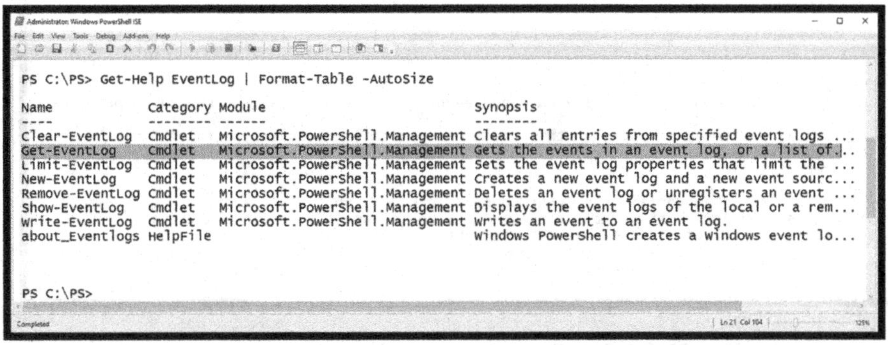

Figure 3-1. *CmdLets referring to the keyword EventLog*

After reviewing the Synopsis, Get-EventLog seems to be a likely target
CmdLet for acquiring events from event logs.

Figure 3-2 displays the basic help information and usage associated
with the Get-EventLog CmdLet.

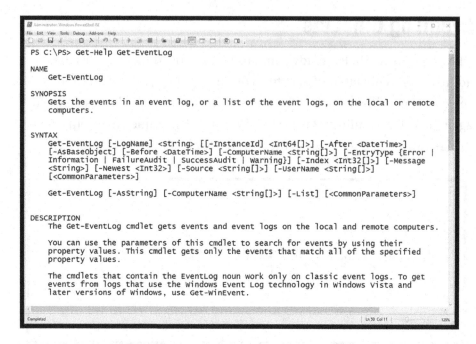

Figure 3-2. *Get-Help Get-EventLog results*

Figure 3-3 depicts several usage examples. Each identifies a different log file and requests the newest 20 events. Note that if the *security* event log is requested, you must have administrative privileges in order to access this.

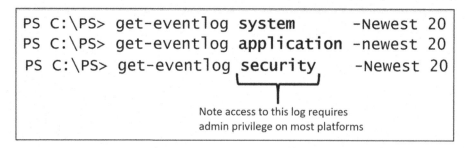

Figure 3-3. *Sample Get-EventLog requests*

·Retrieving More Specific Eventlog Information

Figure 3-4 shows the results after the execution of Get-EventLog.

```
Get-EventLog -logName system -Newest 20
```

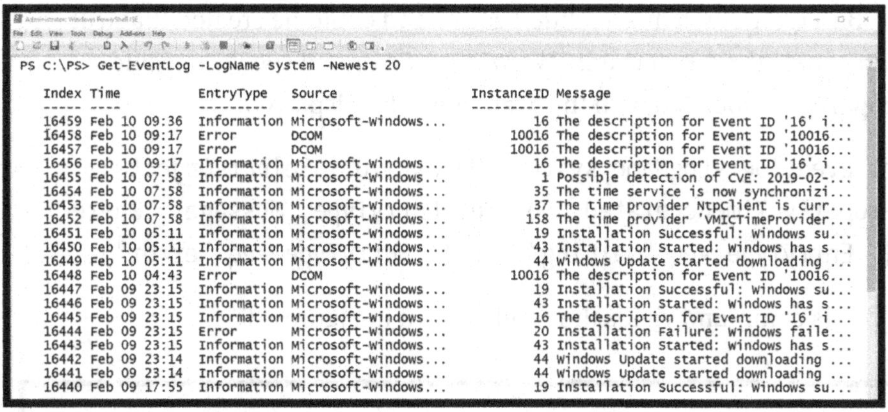

Figure 3-4. *Get-EventLog sample results*   ·

Based on what we learned in Chapter 2 regarding PowerShell pipelining, we can perform more specific or targeted acquisitions of event log data. For example, what if we only want to see events that are of type *error* or *warning* and filter out the general informational messages?

Taking into consideration the excerpt of the Get-Help Get-EventLog result shown in Figure 3-5, the possible EntryTypes listed are:

- Error

- Information

- FailureAudit

- SuccessAudit

- Warning

```
SYNTAX
    Get-EventLog [-LogName] <String> [[-InstanceId] <Int64[]>] [-After <DateTime>] [-AsBaseObject]
    [-Before <DateTime>] [-ComputerName <String[]>] [-EntryType {Error | Information | FailureAudit |
    SuccessAudit | Warning}] [-Index <Int32[]>] [-Message <String>] [-Newest <Int32>] [-Source <String[]>]
    [-UserName <String[]>] [<CommonParameters>]

    Get-EventLog [-AsString] [-ComputerName <String[]>] [-List] [<CommonParameters>]
```

Figure 3-5. *Get-Help excerpt for Get-EventLog*

Based on this, a more refined command could be created that will extract only the target events *Warning* or *Error* and specify specific properties associated with the event log to be displayed.

```
Get-Eventlog -LogName system -Newest 20 | Select-Object
-Property TimeGenerated, Source, EntryType, Message | where
{$_.EntryType -eq "warning" -or $_.EntryType -eq "error"}
```

This command yields the result shown in Figure 3-6.

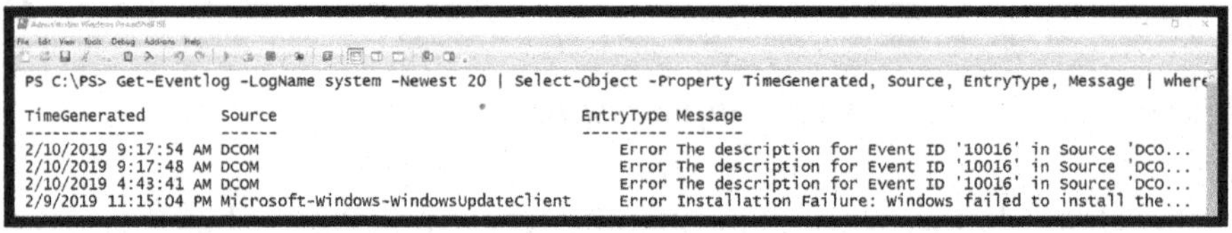

Figure 3-6. *Get-EventLog with specific fields and EntryTypes warning or error*

Creating the Script

Based on this fundamental understanding of Get-EventLog, let's define a challenge problem.

Step One: Define the Challenge

Before you write the script, consider what are the basic challenges that investigators face when retrieving event logs, and how could a PowerShell script be developed that will address these challenges. Ask yourself:

1. What event log or logs need to be collected? Based on the investigation, will specific event log(s) need to be acquired?

2. From what computer or computers should the log files be collected?

3. How many of the most recent records should be collected?

4. Is an optional filter based on *EventType* useful?

5. What specific fields should be generated from the event log?

    - By using Get-Member we can see the common properties of interest include: Category, EntryType, EventID, MachineName, Message, Source, TimeGenerated, TimeWritten and UserName.

6. Where is the output to be generated, that is, the standard output for a file?

7. How will others use the script?

    a. Do we need to provide help?

    b. How will they enter the parameters?

Once you have identified the challenges and are able to answer them, you will now have a working definition for your script and can proceed to step two.

Step Two: Create the Script in Stages

Based on the definition created in Step One, specific parameters need to be defined for our script:

- TargetLog

- TargetComputer

- TargetCount

- TargetEntryType

- ReportTitle

Listing 3-1 shows the complete EventProcessor script. I'll also show the Get-Help results, the sample execution, and the resulting report later on.

Listing 3-1. EventProcessor Script

```
<#
.synopsis
EventProcessor EventLog Capture Automation Version 1.0

- User Specified Target EventLog
- User Specifies the number of newest Log Entries to Report
- User Specifies the Entry Type to target, for example warning,
  error, information etc.
- User Specifies the target computer or computers to extract
  the logs
- User Specifies the HTML Report Title

The script will produce an HTML output file containing details
of the EventLog acquisition.

.Description
This script automates the extraction of information from the
specified log file
```

.parameter targetLogName
Specifies the name of the log file to process
.parameter eventCount
Specifies the maximum number of newest events to consider in
the search
.parameter eventType
Specifies the eventType of interest
.parameter targetComputer
Specifies the computer or computers to obtain the logs from
.parameter reportTitle
Specifies the HTML Report Title

.example
EventProcessor
Execution of EventProcessor without parameters uses the default
settings of
eventLog system
eventType warning
eventCount 20
targetComputer the computer running the script

.example
EventProcessor -targetLogName security
This example specifies the target eventLog security
and uses the default parameters
eventType warning
eventCount 20
targetComputer the computer running the script

.example
EventProcessor -reporTitle "ACME Computer Daily Event Log
Report"
This example provides a custom Report Title

```
.example
EventProcessor -targetLogName security -eventCount 20
-entryType warning -targetComputer Python-3
This example specifies all the parameters, targetLogName,
eventCount, entryType and targetComputer
#>

# Parameter Definition Section
param(
    [string]$targetLogName = "system",
    [int]$eventCount = 20,
    [string]$eventType="Error",
    [string]$reportTitle="Event Log Daily Report",
    [string[]]$targetComputer=$env:COMPUTERNAME
)

# Get the current date and tme
$rptDate=Get-Date
$epoch=([DateTimeOffset]$rptDate).ToUnixTimeSeconds()

# Create HTML Header Section
$Header = @"
<style>
TABLE {border-width: 1px; border-style: solid; border-color:
black; border-collapse: collapse;}
TD {border-width: 1px; padding: 3px; border-style: solid;
border-color: black;}
</style>
<p>
<b> $reportTitle $rptDate </b>
<p>
Event Log Selection: <b>$targetLogName </b>
<p>
```

```
Target Computer(s) Selection: <b> $targetComputer </b>
<p>
Event Type Filter: <b> $eventType </b>
<p>
"@

# Report Filename Creation
$ReportFile = ".\Report-"+$epoch+".HTML"

# CmdLet Pipeline execution
Get-Eventlog -ComputerName $targetComputer -LogName
$targetLogName -Newest $eventCount -EntryType $eventType |
 ConvertTo-HTML -Head $Header -Property TimeGenerated,
EntryType, Message |
 Out-File $ReportFile
```

The EventProcessor script is broken down into four major sections.
The development of PowerShell scripts should include each of these
sections for completeness.

1. Script Header (including Help and Examples)

2. Parameter Definition

3. Local Variable Definition

4. CmdLet Execution Using Parameters and Local
    Variables

Let's take a deeper look at the script construction.

Note   You can use this sample as a baseline since it provides a good
boilerplate for a PowerShell script.

Script Header

The script header contains key information used to define the script and conforms to a strict format in order to deliver help details when processed by the Get-Help CmdLet.

.Synopsis Section

The .synopsis section provides a quick overview of the purpose of the script and what is expected from the user (Listing 3-2).

Listing 3-2. .Synopsis Section

```
<#
.synopsis
EventProcessor EventLog Capture Automation Version 1.0

- User Specified Target EventLog
- User Specifies the number of newest Log Entries to Report
- User Specifies the Entry Type to target, for example warning,
  error, information etc.
- User Specifies the target computer or computers to extract
  the logs
- User Specifies the HTML Report Title

The script will produce an HTML output file containing details
of the EventLog acquisition.
```

.Description Section

The .description section provides a succinct definition of the script (Listing 3-3).

Listing 3-3. .Description Section

```
.Description
This script automates the extraction of information from the
specified log file
```

.Parameters Section

This section defines of each command line parameter utilized by the script in detail (Listing 3-4).

Listing 3-4. .Parameters Section

```
.parameter targetLogName
Specifies the name of the log file to process
.parameter eventCount
Specifies the maximum number of newest events to consider in
the search
.parameter eventType
Specifies the eventType of interest
.parameter targetComputer
Specifies the computer or computers to obtain the logs from
.parameter reportTitle
Specifies the HTML Report Title
```

Note that in this script, all the parameters are optional since during the definition, as you will see later, the default values for each parameter are provided. This allows the user to execute the script by typing:

```
.\EventProcessor
```

.Examples Section

In this section several sample script command line executions are provided along with a definition of what each variant provides (Listing 3-5).

Listing 3-5. .Examples Section

```
.example
EventProcessor
Execution of EventProcessor without parameters uses the default
settings of
eventLog system
eventType warning
eventCount 20
targetComputer the computer running the script

.example
EventProcessor -targetLogName security
This example specifies the target eventLog security
and uses the default parameters
eventType warning
eventCount 20
targetComputer the computer running the script

.example
EventProcessor -reporTitle "ACME Computer Daily Event Log
Report"
This example provides a custom Report Title

.example
EventProcessor -targetLogName security -eventCount 20
-entryType warning -targetComputer Python-3
This example specifies all the parameters, targetLogName,
eventCount, entryType and targetComputer
#>
```

Parameter Definition

The parameter definition section of the script defines the details of each available parameter for the script (Listing 3-6).

Listing 3-6. Parameter Definition Section

```
# Parameter Definition Section
param(
    [string]$targetLogName = "system",
    [int]$eventCount = 20,
    [string]$eventType="Error",
    [string]$reportTitle="Event Log Daily Report",
    [string[]]$targetComputer=$env:COMPUTERNAME
)
```

Each parameter defines a type, name, and the default value assigned. For example:

- The $reportTitle parameter is of type string and has a default value of "Event Log Daily Report".

- The $targetComputer parameter is also of type string, but a set of values is possible. In other words, the user could enter multiple computer names, each separated by a comma. This also contains a default value. This is a PowerShell automatic variable that defines the name of the computer the script is executing on.

- The $targetLogName parameter defines the event log to be targeted. Note that this could have been defined as with $targetComputer to accept a list of log names. However, the standard CmdLet Get-EventLog only supports a single target log. To support a list, the Get-EventLog CmdLet would need to be executed multiple times once for each identified log. This would certainly make the script more complicated, but also potentially even more useful.

- The $EventType parameter allows for the specification of what event type the report should contain. In other words, filter in just the desired event type.

- Finally, the $eventCount parameter is defined as an integer value. It specifies the maximum number of log entries to display that meet the criteria specified.

Local Variable Definition

The local variable section is used to create a few local variables needed for this script (Listing 3-7).

Listing 3-7. Local Variable Definition Section

```
# Get the current date and tme
$rptDate=Get-Date
$epoch=([DateTimeOffset]$rptDate).ToUnixTimeSeconds()

# Create HTML Header Section
$Header = @"
<style>
TABLE {border-width: 1px; border-style: solid; border-color:
black; border-collapse: collapse;}
TD {border-width: 1px; padding: 3px; border-style: solid;
border-color: black;}
</style>
<p>
<b> $reportTitle $rptDate </b>
<p>
```

```
Event Log Selection: <b>$targetLogName </b>
<p>
Target Computer(s) Selection: <b> $targetComputer </b>
<p>
Event Type Filter: <b> $eventType </b>
<p>
"@

# Report Filename Creation
$ReportFile = ".\Report-"+$epoch+".HTML"
```

The local variables are as follows:

- $ReportDate: Obtains the current system date to be
  used in the report.

- $epoch: Obtains the number of seconds that have
  elapsed since the current epoch. Note that this is
  different for each operating system. This variable will
  be used to create a unique HTML filename.

- $Header: Defines a standard HTML header section to
  be used when generating the resulting HTML file. Note
  that this variable uses the parameter ReportTitle in
  order to customize the report heading.

- $ReportFile: This variable combines the string
  "Report-" with the epoch value and the extension
  .html.

CmdLet Pipeline Execution

The core of the script is the execution of the Get-EventLog CmdLet using a
pipeline to include the parameters specified (Listing 3-8).

Listing 3-8. CmdLet Pipeline Execution

```
# CmdLet Pipeline execution
Get-Eventlog -ComputerName $targetComputer -LogName
$targetLogName -Newest $eventCount -EntryType $eventType |
 ConvertTo-html -Head $Header -Property TimeGenerated,
EntryType, Message |
 Out-File $ReportFile
```

The pipeline has several key components and transitions:

1. The Get-EventLog CmdLet specifies the
   -ComputerName, -LogName, -Newest and
   EntryType using the parameters $targetComputer,
   $targetLogName, $eventCount, and $eventType.

2. The output of the Get-EventLog CmdLet is piped
   to the ConvertTo-html CmdLet which utilizes the
   local variable $Header, and the properties passed
   from the Get-EventLog CmdLet TimeGenerated,
   EntryType, and Message to form the columns of the
   HTML report.

3. Finally, the output from ConvertTo-html is piped to
   the Out-File CmdLet which utilizes the local variable
   $ReportFile as the filename to write the results.

EventProcessor Get-Help Result

Since the script contains a detailed header section it is possible to use the
Get-Help CmdLet to provide help to those who will be using the newly
created script. The following example provides the output from the
Get-Help CmdLet using the -Full option which provides all the details
and examples (Listing 3-9).

Listing 3-9. EventProcessor Get-Help

PS C:\PS> Get-Help .\EventProcessor.ps1 -Full

NAME

    C:\PS\EventProcessor.ps1

SYNOPSIS

    EventLog Automation Version 1.0

    Step One

    - User Specified Target EventLog

    - User Specifies the number of newest Log Entries to Report

    - User Specifies the Entry Type to target, for example warning, error, information etc.

    - User Specifies the target computer or computers to extract the logs

    - User Specifies the HTML Report Title

SYNTAX

    C:\PS\EventProcessor.ps1 [[-targetLogName] <String>] [[-eventCount] <Int32>] [[-eventType] <String>] [[-reportTitle] <String>] [[-targetComputer] <String[]>] [<CommonParameters>]

DESCRIPTION

    This script automates the extraction of information from the specified log file

PARAMETERS

    -targetLogName <String>

        Specifies the name of the log file to process

        Required?   false

        Position?   1

```
    Default value               system
    Accept pipeline input?      false
    Accept wildcard characters? false

-eventCount <Int32>
    Specifies the maximum number of newest events to
    consider in the search

    Required?                   false
    Position?                   2
    Default value               20
    Accept pipeline input?      false
    Accept wildcard characters? false

-eventType <String>
    Specifies the eventType of interest

    Required?                   false
    Position?                   3
    Default value               Error
    Accept pipeline input?      false
    Accept wildcard characters? false

-reportTitle <String>
    Specifies the HTML Report Title

    Required?                   false
    Position?                   4
    Default value               Event Log Daily Report
    Accept pipeline input?      false
    Accept wildcard characters? false
```

```
-targetComputer <String[]>
    Specifies the computer or computers to obtain the
    logs from

    Required?                    false
    Position?                    5
    Default value                $env:COMPUTERNAME
    Accept pipeline input?       false
    Accept wildcard characters?  false

<CommonParameters>
    This cmdlet supports the common parameters: Verbose,
    Debug, ErrorAction, ErrorVariable, WarningAction,
    WarningVariable, OutBuffer, PipelineVariable, and
    OutVariable. For more information, see about_Common
    Parameters (https:/go.microsoft.com/fwlink/?LinkID=113216).
```

INPUTS

OUTPUTS

```
----------------------- EXAMPLE 1 -----------------------

PS C:\>EventProcessor

Execution of EventProcessor without parameters uses the
default settings of
eventLog system
eventType warning
eventCount 20
targetComputer the computer running the script
```

```
----------------------- EXAMPLE 2 -----------------------

PS C:\>EventProcessor -targetLogName security

This example specifies the target eventLog security
and uses the default parameters
eventType warning
eventCount 20
targetComputer the computer running the script

----------------------- EXAMPLE 3 -----------------------

PS C:\>EventProcessor -reporTitle "ACME Computer Daily
Event Log Report"

This example provides a custom Report Title

----------------------- EXAMPLE 4 -----------------------

PS C:\>EventProcessor -targetLogName security -eventCount
20 -entryType warning -targetComputer Python-3

This example specifies all the parameters, targetLogName,
eventCount, entryType and targetComputer
```

EventProcessor Script Execution

To illustrate the script execution, a sample command and results are
provided here:

```
PS C:\PS> .\EventProcessor.ps1 -reportTitle "Python Forensics
Daily Log Report" -eventCount 100 -eventType error
```

Resulting Directory

As designed, the script produces an HTML Report File with the appended Epoch value denoting when the script was executed (see Figure 3-7). Since the .html extension was added, the file system properly identifies the resulting file as a Google Chrome HTML Document.

Figure 3-7. *Resulting report HTML file*

HTML Output Report

Examining the report file `Report-1544369607` using a browser provides sample results from the PowerShell script execution. The output includes the defined report title, the event log that was selected, the target computer, and the event type that was selected along with the resulting last 100 events with an event type of error. Note that the results were truncated here for brevity.

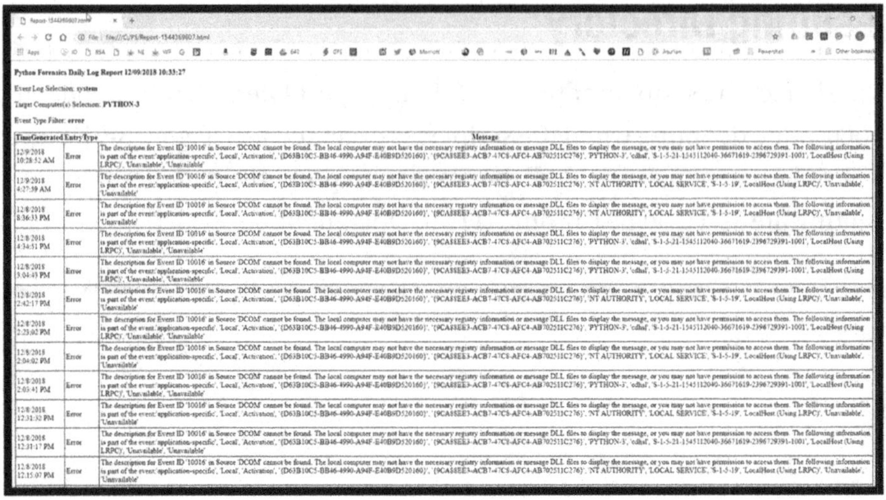

Figure 3-8. Resulting HTML report

Remote Access

Note   Setting up access to remote systems using the
-ComputerName option (that is available for many CmdLets) can
be difficult to setup within a workgroup. It is much easier when a
Domain Controller is present, or your environment utilizes active
directory. So please consult your system administrator when
attempting to use the -ComputerName CmdLet parameter.

There is an easier method that can provide even greater flexibility and is
more secure. The method is to create a remote PowerShell session with
the target machine. Once the session is established, the commands that
you enter from within PowerShell or PowerShell ISE are executed on the
remotely connected machine. The advantage is not only simplicity, but
it also allows you to execute any CmdLet, even those that don't support
-ComputerName as a parameter.

Here is a simple example that creates a PowerShell session with a machine on my local network with the computer name Levovo-Upstairs. In order to create the session, you must provide the credentials for a user on the remote machine with Admin rights. The command will pop up a dialog box requesting the password for the specified account, as shown in Figure 3-9.

Figure 3-9. *Enter-PSSession credential request*

Once the connection is made, you can see that the PowerShell prompt has changed to:

```
[Lenovo-Upstairs]: PS C:\Users\Remote-Admin\Documents>
```

At this point, PowerShell commands that are typed are being executed on the remote computer Lenovo-Upstairs not on the local machine. In the example shown in Figure 3-10, the newest 20 warning messages contained in the system event log on the Lenovo-Upstairs machine are acquired.

```
PS C:\PS> Enter-PSSession -ComputerName Lenovo-Upstairs -Credential Lenovo-Upstairs/Remote-Admin

[Lenovo-Upstairs]: PS C:\Users\Remote-Admin\Documents> Get-EventLog -LogName system -EntryType warning -Newest 20

Index  Time          EntryType  Source              InstanceID Message
-----  ----          ---------  ------              ---------- -------
3632508 Dec 10 12:27  Warning    WinRM                   468901 The description for Event ID '468901' in Source 'WinRM' ca...
3632505 Dec 10 12:25  Warning    WinRM                   468901 The description for Event ID '468901' in Source 'WinRM' ca...
3632500 Dec 10 12:24  Warning    BROWSER             2147491669 The browser service was unable to retrieve a list of serve...
3632492 Dec 10 12:11  Warning    Microsoft-Windows...       219 The driver \Driver\WudfRd failed to load for the device SW...
3632400 Dec 10 11:57  Warning    WinRM                   468901 The description for Event ID '468901' in Source 'WinRM' ca...
3632375 Dec 10 03:29  Warning    Microsoft-Windows...       134 NtpClient was unable to set a manual peer to use as a time...
3632350 Dec 09 14:14  Warning    Microsoft-Windows...        16 Unable to Connect: Windows is unable to connect to the aut...
3632328 Dec 09 02:06  Warning    Microsoft-Windows...       134 NtpClient was unable to set a manual peer to use as a time...


[Lenovo-Upstairs]: PS C:\Users\Remote-Admin\Documents> Exit-PSSession

PS C:\PS>
```

Figure 3-10. *Remote access of the system event log*

To exit the remote session the CmdLet Exit-PSSession is issued and PowerShell is now back operating on the local machine again. This is shown in Figure 3-10.

Example 2: USB Device Usage Discovery

Obtaining the recent USB devices used can certainly be important when performing forensic investigations or incident response actions. This can either help determine if information was exfiltrated from the system, or if USB insertion could be the cause of malware infection.

The first part of that process is to determine what USB devices have been detected. On Microsoft Windows systems, the registry provides a history of devices attached by examining details kept under HKEY_Local_ Machine. Figure 3-11 shows the specific USBSTOR keys found on my local machine.

Note   On different versions of Windows the registry key of interest may be different. If so, you will need to change the registry key definitions used in this example.

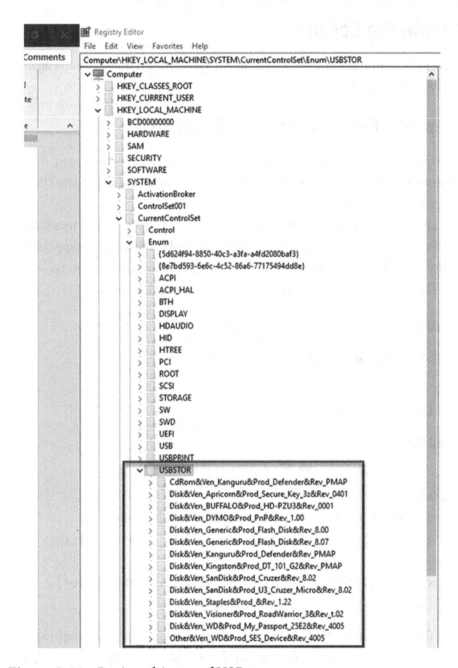

Figure 3-11. *Registry history of USB access*

Create the Script

Now that we understand the scenario, let's go through the two steps again to create the script we need.

Step One: Recent Accessing USB Activity

The question is how can evidence of USB activity be collected using PowerShell? Also, could a script be developed that would aggregate USB usage across our network?

Let's start by accessing the registry and USBSTOR on a local machine.

PowerShell provides a general-purpose CmdLet that can be applied to many items including the registry: The CmdLet is Get-ItemProperty.

The Get-Help for Get-ItemProperty is shown in Listing 3-10.

Listing 3-10. Get-Help Get-ItemProperty

```
PS C:\PS> Get-Help Get-ItemProperty

NAME
    Get-ItemProperty

SYNOPSIS
    Gets the properties of a specified item.

SYNTAX
    Get-ItemProperty [[-Name] <String[]>] [-Credential
    <PSCredential>] [-Exclude <String[]>] [-Filter <String>]
    [-Include
    <String[]>] -LiteralPath <String[]> [-UseTransaction]
    [<CommonParameters>]

    Get-ItemProperty [-Path] <String[]> [[-Name] <String[]>]
    [-Credential <PSCredential>] [-Exclude <String[]>] [-Filter
```

<String>] [-Include <String[]>] [-UseTransaction]
[<CommonParameters>]

DESCRIPTION

The Get-ItemProperty cmdlet gets the properties of the
specified items. For example, you can use this cmdlet to
get the value
of the LastAccessTime property of a file object. **You can
also use this cmdlet to view registry entries and their
values.**

RELATED LINKS

Online Version: http://go.microsoft.com/fwlink/?LinkId=821588
Clear-ItemProperty
Copy-ItemProperty
Move-ItemProperty
New-ItemProperty
Remove-ItemProperty
Rename-ItemProperty
Set-ItemProperty

REMARKS

To see the examples, type: "get-help Get-ItemProperty
-examples".
For more information, type: "get-help Get-ItemProperty
-detailed".
For technical information, type: "get-help Get-ItemProperty
-full".
For online help, type: "get-help Get-ItemProperty -online"

Using this CmdLet to acquire recent USB activity can be accomplished like this. In order to make this easier to understand, for this example the "Friendly Name" Property of the USB device will be acquired. Please see Figure 3-12.

PS C:\PS> **Get-ItemProperty -Path HKLM:\SYSTEM\ CurrentControlSet\Enum\USBSTOR** | Select FriendlyName**

Figure 3-12. *Using Get-ItemProperty CmdLet to acquire USB activity*

Using the Remote Access method, we now acquire the USB activity on the remote computer Lenovo-Upstairs. For this, the Enter and Exit PSSession method is used and the command is executed on the remote computer. As you can see, the SanDisk Cruzer USB device was identified on both the local and remote computers.

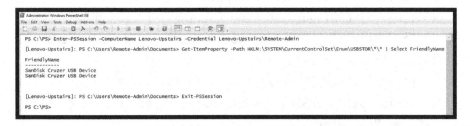

Figure 3-13. Access USB activity on a remote computer

Invoke-Command PowerShell CmdLet

In cases where only a single remote command needs to be executed, this can be accomplished by using the Invoke-Command PowerShell CmdLet instead of setting up a remote PowerShell session. This can be useful when developing scripts that will acquire evidence from multiple computers. As always using Get-Help will provide the details on how to utilize the Invoke-Command CmdLet (Listing 3-11).

Listing 3-11. Invoke-Command

```
PS C:\PS> Get-Help Invoke-Command

NAME
    Invoke-Command

SYNOPSIS
    Runs commands on local and remote computers.

SYNTAX
```

75

```
Invoke-Command [[-ConnectionUri] <Uri[]>] [-ScriptBlock]
<ScriptBlock> [-AllowRedirection] [-ArgumentList
<Object[]>] [-AsJob]
[-Authentication {Default | Basic | Negotiate |
NegotiateWithImplicitCredential | Credssp | Digest |
Kerberos}] [-CertificateThumbprint
<String>] [-ConfigurationName <String>] [-Credential
<PSCredential>] [-EnableNetworkAccess] [-HideComputerName]
[-InDisconnectedSession]
[-InputObject <PSObject>] [-JobName <String>]
[-SessionOption <PSSessionOption>] [-ThrottleLimit <Int32>]
[<CommonParameters>]

Invoke-Command [[-ConnectionUri] <Uri[]>] [-FilePath]
<String> [-AllowRedirection] [-ArgumentList <Object[]>]
[-AsJob] [-Authentication
{Default | Basic | Negotiate |
NegotiateWithImplicitCredential | Credssp | Digest |
Kerberos}] [-ConfigurationName <String>] [-Credential
<PSCredential>] [-EnableNetworkAccess] [-HideComputerName]
[-InDisconnectedSession] [-InputObject <PSObject>]
[-JobName <String>]
[-SessionOption <PSSessionOption>] [-ThrottleLimit <Int32>]
[<CommonParameters>]

Invoke-Command [[-ComputerName] <String[]>] [-ScriptBlock]
<ScriptBlock> [-ApplicationName <String>] [-ArgumentList
<Object[]>] [-AsJob]
[-Authentication {Default | Basic | Negotiate |
NegotiateWithImplicitCredential | Credssp | Digest |
Kerberos}] [-CertificateThumbprint
```

```
<String>] [-ConfigurationName <String>] [-Credential
<PSCredential>] [-EnableNetworkAccess] [-HideComputerName]
[-InDisconnectedSession]
[-InputObject <PSObject>] [-JobName <String>] [-Port
<Int32>] [-SessionName <String[]>] [-SessionOption
<PSSessionOption>] [-ThrottleLimit
<Int32>] [-UseSSL] [<CommonParameters>]

Invoke-Command [[-ComputerName] <String[]>] [-FilePath]
<String> [-ApplicationName <String>] [-ArgumentList
<Object[]>] [-AsJob]
[-Authentication {Default | Basic | Negotiate |
NegotiateWithImplicitCredential | Credssp | Digest |
Kerberos}] [-ConfigurationName
<String>] [-Credential <PSCredential>]
[-EnableNetworkAccess] [-HideComputerName]
[-InDisconnectedSession] [-InputObject <PSObject>]
[-JobName <String>] [-Port <Int32>] [-SessionName
<String[]>] [-SessionOption <PSSessionOption>]
[-ThrottleLimit <Int32>] [-UseSSL]
[<CommonParameters>]

Invoke-Command [[-Session] <PSSession[]>] [-ScriptBlock]
<ScriptBlock> [-ArgumentList <Object[]>] [-AsJob]
[-HideComputerName]
[-InputObject <PSObject>] [-JobName <String>]
[-ThrottleLimit <Int32>] [<CommonParameters>]

Invoke-Command [[-Session] <PSSession[]>] [-FilePath]
<String> [-ArgumentList <Object[]>] [-AsJob]
[-HideComputerName] [-InputObject
<PSObject>] [-JobName <String>] [-ThrottleLimit <Int32>]
[<CommonParameters>]
```

```
Invoke-Command [-VMId] <Guid[]> [-ScriptBlock]
<ScriptBlock> [-ArgumentList <Object[]>] [-AsJob]
[-ConfigurationName <String>] -Credential
<PSCredential> [-HideComputerName] [-InputObject
<PSObject>] [-ThrottleLimit <Int32>] [<CommonParameters>]

Invoke-Command [-ScriptBlock] <ScriptBlock> [-ArgumentList
<Object[]>] [-AsJob] [-ConfigurationName <String>]
-Credential <PSCredential>
[-HideComputerName] [-InputObject <PSObject>]
[-ThrottleLimit <Int32>] -VMName <String[]>
[<CommonParameters>]

Invoke-Command [-VMId] <Guid[]> [-FilePath] <String>
[-ArgumentList <Object[]>] [-AsJob] [-ConfigurationName
<String>] -Credential
<PSCredential> [-HideComputerName] [-InputObject
<PSObject>] [-ThrottleLimit <Int32>] [<CommonParameters>]

Invoke-Command [-FilePath] <String> [-ArgumentList
<Object[]>] [-AsJob] [-ConfigurationName <String>]
-Credential <PSCredential>
[-HideComputerName] [-InputObject <PSObject>]
[-ThrottleLimit <Int32>] -VMName <String[]>
[<CommonParameters>]

Invoke-Command [-ScriptBlock] <ScriptBlock> [-ArgumentList
<Object[]>] [-AsJob] [-ConfigurationName <String>]
-ContainerId <String[]>
[-HideComputerName] [-InputObject <PSObject>] [-JobName
<String>] [-RunAsAdministrator] [-ThrottleLimit <Int32>]
[<CommonParameters>]
```

```
Invoke-Command [-FilePath] <String> [-ArgumentList
<Object[]>] [-AsJob] [-ConfigurationName <String>]
-ContainerId <String[]>
[-HideComputerName] [-InputObject <PSObject>] [-JobName
<String>] [-RunAsAdministrator] [-ThrottleLimit <Int32>]
[<CommonParameters>]

Invoke-Command [-ScriptBlock] <ScriptBlock> [-ArgumentList
<Object[]>] [-InputObject <PSObject>] [-NoNewScope]
[<CommonParameters>]
```

DESCRIPTION

The Invoke-Command cmdlet runs commands on a local or remote computer and returns all output from the commands, including errors. By using a single Invoke-Command command, you can run commands on multiple computers.

To run a single command on a remote computer, use the ComputerName parameter. To run a series of related commands that share data, use the New-PSSession cmdlet to create a PSSession (a persistent connection) on the remote computer, and then use the Session parameter of Invoke-Command to run the command in the PSSession. To run a command in a disconnected session, use the InDisconnectedSession parameter. To run a command in a background job, use the AsJob parameter.

You can also use Invoke-Command on a local computer to evaluate or run a string in a script block as a command. Windows PowerShell converts the script block to a command and runs the command immediately in the current scope, instead of just echoing the string at the command line.

To start an interactive session with a remote computer, use the Enter-PSSession cmdlet. To establish a persistent connection to a remote computer, use the New-PSSession cmdlet.

Before using Invoke-Command to run commands on a remote computer, read about_Remote (http://go.microsoft.com/ fwlink/?LinkID=135182).

RELATED LINKS
Online Version: http://go.microsoft.com/fwlink/?LinkId=821493
Enter-PSSession
Exit-PSSession
Get-PSSession
New-PSSession
Remove-PSSession

Using the USB activity acquisition method as a starting point, the Invoke-Command method can be used to perform this command remotely. In this example, target and user are first created as variables. The command is embedded in the -ScriptBlock. As before, the user must enter the Admin credentials for the remote computer (Figure 3-14).

Figure 3-14. *Invoke-Command method USBAcquire*

The results to the Invoke command are shown in Figure 3-15.

Figure 3-15. *Invoke-Command method USBAcquire results*

Step Two: Create the USBAcquire PowerShell Script

Now that we have perfected the method, a simple PowerShell script can be created to perform this operation for us, with the user supplying the target computer name and the Admin user. The full script is listed here as Listing 3-12. I'll show the Get-Help result and a sample execution later as well.

Listing 3-12. USBAcquire Script

```
<#
.synopsis
Collect USB Activity from target computer

- User Specifies the target computer

The script will produce details of USB Activity
on the specified target computer

.Description
This script collects USB Activity and target computers

.parameter targetComputer
Specifies the computer to collect the USB Activity

.parameter UserName
Specifies the Administrator UserName on the Target Computer

.example

USBAcquire ComputerName
Collects the USB Activity on the target Computer
#>

# Parameter Definition Section
param(
    [string]$User,
    [string]$targetComputer
)

Invoke-Command -ComputerName $targetComputer -Credential
$User -ScriptBlock {Get-ItemProperty -Path HKLM:\SYSTEM\
CurrentControlSet\Enum\USBSTOR\*\* | Select FriendlyName}
```

As you can see, the USBAcquire has the same four major sections as the EventProcessor script from Example One: Script Header parameter definition, Local variable definitions, and cmdlet execution using parameters and local variables. Refer back to that section if you need a refresher.

USBAcquire Script Execution

The execution and results of the script are demonstrated in Figures 3-16 and 3-17.

```
PS C:\PS> .\USBAcquire.ps1 -targetComputer PYTHON-3 -user
PYTHON-3\USER-NAME-HIDDEN
```

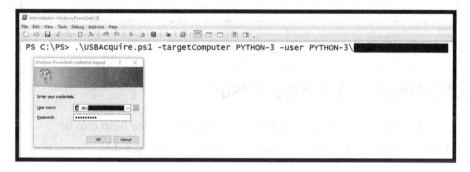

Figure 3-16. USBAcquire script execution requesting credentials

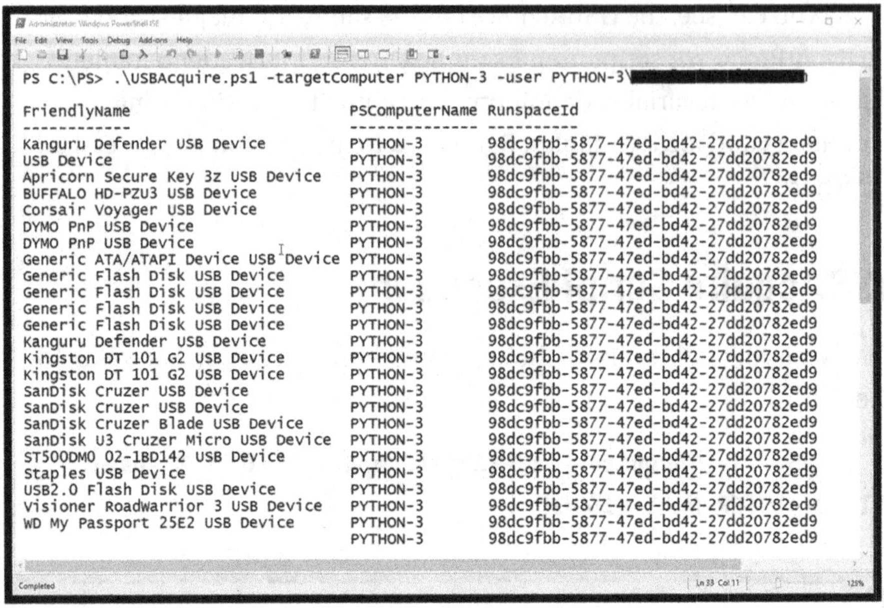

Figure 3-17. *Results USBAcquire PowerShell script*

USBAcquire Get-Help Result

The script contains a proper heading section; thus, user help can be obtained using the Get-Help CmdLet, shown in Listing 3-13.

Listing 3-13. USBAcquire Get-Help

```
PS C:\PS> Get-Help .\USBAcquire.ps1

NAME
    C:\PS\USBAcquire.ps1

SYNOPSIS
    Collect USB Activity from target computer

    - User Specifies the target computer
```

The script will produce details of USB Activity
on the specified target computer

SYNTAX
  C:\PS\USBAcquire.ps1 [[-User] <String>] [[-targetComputer]
  <String>] [<CommonParameters>]

DESCRIPTION
  This script collects USB Activity and target computers

RELATED LINKS

REMARKS
  To see the examples, type: "get-help C:\PS\USBAcquire.ps1
  -examples".
  For more information, type: "get-help C:\PS\USBAcquire.ps1
  -detailed".
  For technical information, type: "get-help C:\PS\
  USBAcquire.ps1 -full".

Challenge Problem: Create File Inventory List with Hashes

Based on what you have learned about PowerShell scripts and Remote
Access methods, your challenge is to leverage this knowledge to solve the
following problem.

Develop a PowerShell script that will create an inventory of a computer
detailing all directories and files found. The script will allow the user to
specify:

- Target Computer

- Starting Directory

- Output File

Your script should produce an HTML file that contains the following information:

- Directory

- FileName

- FileSize

- LastWriteTime

- Owner

- FileAttributes (i.e., ReadOnly, Hidden, System, Archive)

The script will recurse all the folders beginning with the Starting Directory.

Hint   You will be focusing on the CmdLet Get-ChildItem.

Finally, your script will contain full Help information.

A sample script solution can be found in Appendix A and at www.apress.com/9781484245033.

Summary

This chapter focused on the construction of PowerShell scripts that can be used by investigators to obtain information from event logs and recent USB activity. The Get-EventLog CmdLet and Get-ItemProperty were the focus of our acquisitions.

In addition, the creation of PowerShell sessions was covered as an additional method to obtain evidence from remote computers when proper credentials are available using the Enter-PSSession CmdLet. Also, the Invoke-Command PowerShell CmdLet was covered that allows for the execution of a single command or script without creating a persistent session.

Chapter 4 will introduce, compare, and contrast PowerShell and Python and begin the process of combining these two powerful scripting languages.

CHAPTER 4

Python and Live Investigation/ Acquisition

Searching is the mainstay of digital investigation. What has changed over the past decade is the vast amount of data to search, the various types of content to search, and the type of information that is needed to connect the dots of specific criminal activity.

Today, digital data is connected to all criminal activity. Using this data to understand (and potentially prove) the motive, opportunity, and/or means to commit the crime is paramount. In many cases, we can utilize this data to develop a profile of a suspect(s) and predict future activities. In addition, we can discover the location, behaviors, and content of specific digital devices whether they be phones, tablets, computers, drones, watches, or a wide range of IoT devices.

Currently, many still think about digital evidence as static data that is examined after we image digital media. This is changing of course, especially in Digital Forensic Incident Response, or DFIR, activities. Collecting, examining, and reasoning about "live" evidence is not new – I began writing about this and developing solutions as far back as 2006.[1]

---

[1] https://gcn.com/Articles/2006/07/27/Special-Report%2D%2DLive-forensics-is-the-future-for-law-enforcement.aspx

© Chet Hosmer 2019
C. Hosmer, *PowerShell and Python Together*, https://doi.org/10.1007/978-1-4842-4504-0_4

As the need for immediate response, early indications and warning, detection of aberrant behavior, and anticipation of bad actions before they occur becomes vital in society, "live" forensics will eventually work hand in hand with traditional postmortem practices. Thus, by leveraging PowerShell to acquire specific targeted evidence, we can take the next step in processing and reasoning about actions as they happen.

All of this provides significant opportunities to develop new methods of detection, reasoning, analysis, and of course evidence of criminal activity. However, before we can fly, run, walk, or even crawl, we need to tackle some basic challenges and develop software that integrates PowerShell-driven acquisition with the power of Python. There are two fundamental ways to approach this:

- Method 1: Launch PowerShell CmdLets or scripts and then collect and post-process the results in Python.

- Method 2: Execute PowerShell CmdLets or scripts and pipe the results to waiting Python scripts.

Method 1 will be examined in this chapter and Method 2 will be addressed in Chapter 5. In both cases, the methods will be explored by example.

What Is "By Example"?

There are literally hundreds of books on Python in existence, and most are focused on how to program and typically take the approach of teaching you the intricacies of the language. These texts are designed for those pursuing a career in computer science, software engineering, web development, or Big Data processing.

Our goal here is to apply Python to specific digital investigation challenges and combine Python and PowerShell to create solutions. Interestingly enough, along the way you will learn new scripting techniques.

The best analogy I can think of is learning about a new culture. You can read about the Mayan culture, watch movies about their history, and examine maps of the countries where they resided. Or you can travel there and walk through their world, speak with the Maya people, explore their sacred sites, and experience the culture firsthand.

Directing PowerShell with Python

Since the end date of Python 2.7 is approaching, Python 3.7 will be used for all the Python-based examples for this book. Python 2 and 3 contain a formidable amount of built-in standard libraries along with thousands of third-party libraries. Whenever possible, Python standard libraries will be used in order to ensure the broadest cross-platform compatibility. You can obtain Python 3.7 directly from `www.python.org`. As of this writing, the latest version available is Python 3.7.2, as shown in Figure 4-1.

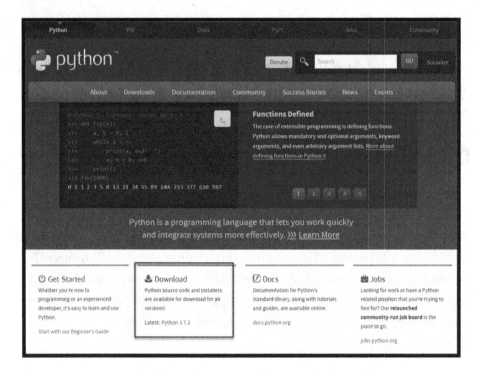

Figure 4-1. *Download Python 3.7.2 (`www.python.org`)*

In addition to the latest version of Python, I highly recommend the use of a Python Integrated Development Environment. My favorite is WingIDE.

The personal edition is free and works fine for most Python development and scripting challenges. The web site provides great tutorials on how to configure and use WingIDE can be found at:

`www.wingware.com`

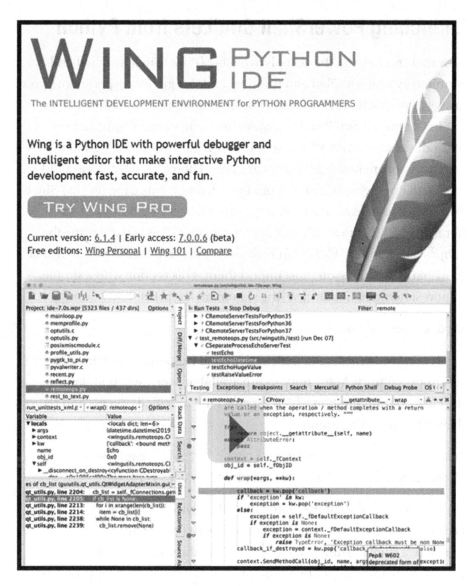

Figure 4-2. *Wingware/WingIDE home page (www.wingware.com)*

Launching PowerShell CmdLets from Python

Now that you have the basic tools available (PowerShell installed and running, Python installed and running, and WingIDE to experiment), you are set to perform the first integration of Python and PowerShell.

In Chapters 1 and 2, the discovery, use, and forensic applications of CmdLets were covered. I'm sure that you have already experimented with an assortment of additional CmdLets. Therefore, what if we could execute a PowerShell CmdLet from Python and capture the results? Since PowerShell is an executable process, so we will use Python's standard library providing the ability to launch processes. This is done using the subprocess standard library. In Python in order to utilize any standard or third-party libraries, you must import them. This is done with a simple import statement. In this case, the statement simply is:

```
import subprocess
```

This provides access to the methods and properties contained in the subprocess library. Many options are available – the most popular is using the check.output method which executes the specified process and returns the result. Here is an example:

```
runningProcesses = subprocess.check_output("powershell
-Executionpolicy ByPass -Command Get-Process")
```

One of the nice features of the WingIDE Python Integrated Development is the ability to experiment with commands within the interactive shell as shown in Figure 4-3. The three greater-than signs (>>>) are the interactive shell prompt. This is the same prompt you would receive if you launched Python from the command line or terminal window.

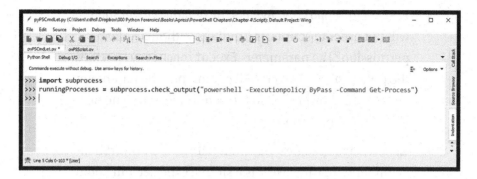

Figure 4-3. *Executing a PowerShell CmdLet from the Python shell*

The breakdown of each of the elements of the subprocess code is as follows and in Figure 4-4.

- **A.** The result of the command will be stored in the variable named `runningProcesses`. You can, of course, use any allowable variable name. I use camel case when defining variables in Python starting with a lowercase letter and then capitalizing each subsequent word. This makes it easy to identify variables in your code.

- **B.** The assignment operator or = equal sign assigns the results of the subprocess command to the variable `runningProcesses`.

- **C.** `subprocess.check_output` is the selected method from the subprocess library. It takes a single parameter enclosed in quotes and defines the command line you wish to execute.

- **D.** The quoted string inside the parenthesis specifies the command to execute. E-H defines each element of the powershell command to execute.

- **E.** `powershell` is the command, or in this case the process to execute.

95

- **F.** `-Executionpolicy ByPass`, by default, PowerShell will not execute scripts or CmdLets without explicit permission. The parameter `-Executionpolicy` specifies the policy for the PowerShell command. The parameter `ByPass` tells PowerShell to block nothing and issue no warnings or prompts.

- **G.** `-Command` specifies that what follows is a PowerShell Command. In this case it is a simple CmdLet, but could be a more complex pipeline-based command. If you desire to execute a PowerShell script, this would be changed to `-File` and would be followed by a valid .ps1 filename.

- **H.** `Get-Process` is the specific CmdLet that is to be executed. In this example the Get-Process CmdLet is executed with no parameters.

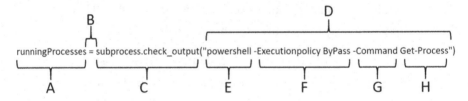

Figure 4-4. *Python subprocess command breakdown*

In Python 3.x, the subprocess.check_output() method returns a byte string, where in Python 2.7 it returned a simple string. Therefore, to display the output from the Command, the runningProcesses variable needs to be decoded as shown here:

```
print(runningProcesses.decode())
```

Executing this command within the WingIDE Python interactive shell delivers the results shown in Figure 4-5. Note the results are truncated for brevity.

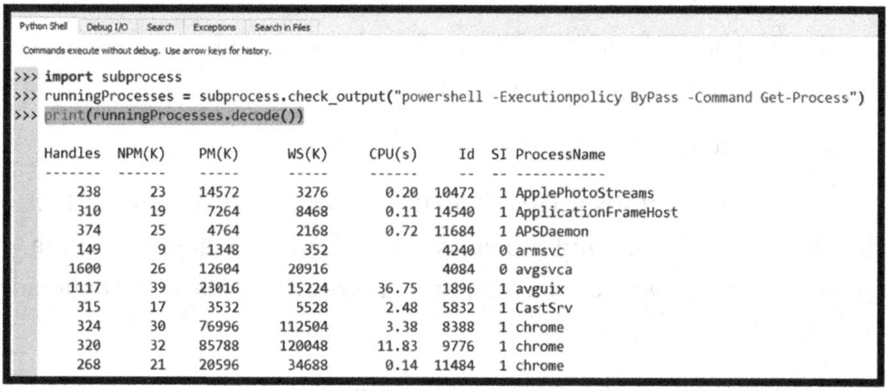

```
Python Shell    Debug I/O    Search    Exceptions    Search in Files

Commands execute without debug. Use arrow keys for history.

>>> import subprocess
>>> runningProcesses = subprocess.check_output("powershell -Executionpolicy ByPass -Command Get-Process")
>>> print(runningProcesses.decode())

Handles  NPM(K)    PM(K)     WS(K)    CPU(s)     Id  SI ProcessName
-------  ------    -----     -----    ------     --  -- -----------
    238      23    14572      3276      0.20  10472   1 ApplePhotoStreams
    310      19     7264      8468      0.11  14540   1 ApplicationFrameHost
    374      25     4764      2168      0.72  11684   1 APSDaemon
    149       9     1348       352               4240   0 armsvc
   1600      26    12604     20916               4084   0 avgsvca
   1117      39    23016     15224     36.75   1896   1 avguix
    315      17     3532      5528      2.48   5832   1 CastSrv
    324      30    76996    112504      3.38   8388   1 chrome
    320      32    85788    120048     11.83   9776   1 chrome
    268      21    20596     34688      0.14  11484   1 chrome
```

Figure 4-5. *Printing out the contents of the runningProcesses variable*

At this point you might be saying why would I go through the trouble to execute a PowerShell Command or CmdLet from Python? In order to answer that question let's take this example to the next level.

Creating a System Files Baseline with PowerShell and Python

Let's say you wish to establish a baseline of what drivers are currently installed under Windows, specifically c:\windows\system32\drivers\. You could target any directory, subdirectories, or the whole system for that matter, but system drivers run with privilege, and detecting new drivers, modifications of existing drivers, or removal of a driver could be useful during an investigation.

Obtaining information regarding files is accomplished using the Get-ChildItem CmdLet within PowerShell. This CmdLet has many features, properties, and methods associated with it. What we are interested in to create the baseline is:

1. The hash of each file for creating a known good hashset used by forensic software

2. The name of each file

It is quite straightforward to obtain this information from PowerShell using the Pipeline command shown as follows. The truncated results are depicted in Figure 4-6 and the command breakdown is described in detail in Figure 4-7.

```
Get-ChildItem c:\windows\system32\drivers\ |
Get-FileHash | Select-object -Property Hash, Path | Format-
Table -HideTableHeaders
```

Figure 4-6. *Obtain file hash and path using PowerShell (note output is truncated)*

The breakdown of the Pipeline command is shown as follows and in Figure 4-7.

- **A.** Get-ChildItem CmdLet specifying the target folder windows\system32\drivers.

- **B.** The output of the Get-ChildItem CmdLet is piped to the Get-FileHash CmdLet which will, by default, generate the SHA-256 hash of each file.

- **C.** The result of the Get-FileHash CmdLet will be piped to the Select-Object CmdLet which will extract just the SHA-256 hash value and the File Path of the two outputs that are needed.

- **D.** The results of the Select-Object CmdLet are then passed to the Format-Table CmdLet which removes the Table Header from the output.

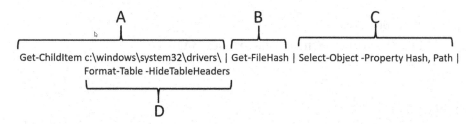

Figure 4-7. *PowerShell Pipeline breakdown Get-ChildItem, Get-FileHash, Select-Object, and Format-Table*

Creating a PowerShell script with input parameters will make this command a bit more useful and re-useable. The complete script is shown in Listing 4-1.

Listing 4-1. HashAquire.ps1 Script

```
<#
.synopsis
Collect Hash and Filenames from specified folder

- User Specifies the target computer
- User Specifies the target folder
```

The script will produce a simple ascii output file containing
SHA-256Hash and FilePath

```
.Description
This script collects Hash and Filenames from specified computer
and folder

.parameter targetComputer
Specifies the computer to collect the specified file hash
information

.parameter UserName
Specifies the Administrator UserName on the Target Computer

.parameter outFile
Specifies the full path of the output file

.example

HashAcquire
Collects the file hashes on the target Computer
#>

# Parameter Definition Section
param(
    [string]$TargetFolder="c:/windows/system32/drivers/",
    [string]$ResultFile="c:/PS/baseline.txt"
)

Get-ChildItem $TargetFolder | Get-FileHash | Select-Object
-Property Hash, Path | Format-Table -HideTableHeaders | Out-
File $ResultFile -Encoding ascii
```

The script has the standard sections in order to provide the proper
Get-Help support, as shown in Listing 4-2.

Listing 4-2. Get-Help Results for the HashAquire.ps1 PowerShell
Script

```
PS C:\PS> Get-Help .\HashAcquire.ps1
NAME
    C:\PS\HashAcquire.ps1

SYNOPSIS
    Collect Hash and Filenames from specified folder

    - User Specifies the target computer
    - User Specifies the target folder

    The script will produce a simple ascii output file
    containing
    SHA-256Hash and FilePath

SYNTAX
    C:\PS\HashAcquire.ps1 [[-TargetFolder] <String>]
    [[-ResultFile] <String>] [<CommonParameters>]

DESCRIPTION
    This script collects Hash and Filenames from specified
    computer and folder

RELATED LINKS

REMARKS
    To see the examples, type: "get-help C:\PS\HashAcquire.ps1
    -examples".
    For more information, type: "get-help C:\PS\HashAcquire.ps1
    -detailed".
    For technical information, type: "get-help C:\PS\
    HashAcquire.ps1 -full".
```

The script contains two input parameters TargetFolder and ResultFile.

```
# Parameter Definition Section
param(
    [string]$TargetFolder="c:/windows/system32/drivers/",
    [string]$ResultFile="c:/PS/baseline.txt"
)
```

Using the default parameters, the script creates the baseline.txt file. The abbreviated results are shown in Figure 4-8. By supplying a parameter for specifying the target folder, this script can now be applied to any legitimate folder.

Note   Access to certain folders will require administrator privilege. Make sure that you are running PowerShell as Admin.

```
PS C:\PS> .\HashAcquire.ps1
```

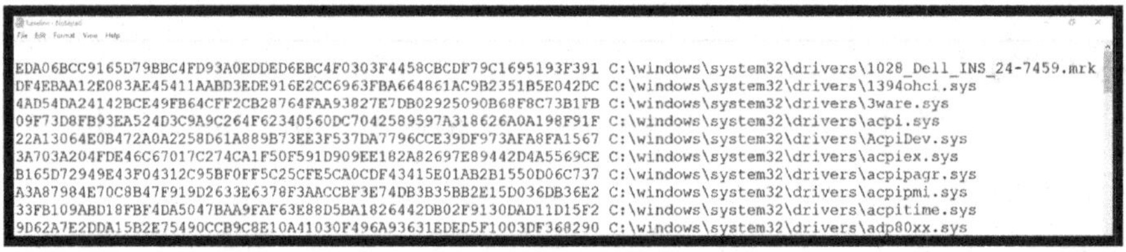

Figure 4-8. baseline.txt abbreviated results

Creating the Baseline with Python

Now that we have a reliable method of extracting the hash and filename using the HashAcquire.ps1 PowerShell script, we can use Python to create a baseline from these results. However, for this we will create a Python script/program instead of using the interactive shell.

The plan is to launch the PowerShell script from Python and extract the results from the created text file. You can specify the name and location of the resulting file by using the ResultFile parameter provided by the script.

Note   The current PowerShell script only processes the specified directory. However, the Get-ChildItem CmdLet has an optional parameter that could be used to specify sub-folder acquisition as well. That parameter is -recurse, by using:

```
Get-Help Get-ChildItem
```

You will find that Get-ChildItem has many options and example usage.

The next step is to store the extracted results in a Python dictionary to produce a baseline. Once the dictionary baseline is created, the resulting dictionary can be stored and used for comparison. This way you can detect any new, modified, or deleted files from a target folder.

Note   Python dictionaries, much like traditional Webster-style dictionaries, have a Key and a Value, which are typically referred to as a Key/Value pair. In Python, both the Key and the Value can be complex, the only rule being that the Key must be a hashable type such as an integer, long, string, or tuple. The Value part of the Key/Value pair can be a list or other nonhashable data type. In addition, the dictionary's keys must be unique (much like real dictionaries).

The complete CreateBaseline.py script is shown in Listing 4-3.

Note   For the PowerShell and Python scripts throughout the rest of the book, the directory c:\PS was created to hold the scripts and results.

Also, do not try to copy and paste the Python scripts from the book text. Python uses a method of strict indentation that can be corrupted through the copy and paste process. The publisher has provided access to the source code files at: www.apress. com/9781484245033.

Listing 4-3. CreateBaseLine Python Script

```
'''
Step One Create a baseline hash list of target folder
December 2018, Python Forensics

'''

''' LIBRARY IMPORT SECTION '''

import subprocess        # subprocess library
import argparse          # argument parsing library
import os                # Operating System Path
import pickle            # Python object serialization

'''ARGUMENT PARSING SECTION '''

def ValidatePath(thePath):
    ''' Validate the Folder thePath
        it must exist and we must have rights
        to read from the folder.
```

```
        raise the appropriate error if either
        is not true
    '''
    # Validate the path exists
    if not os.path.exists(thePath):
        raise argparse.ArgumentTypeError('Path does
        not exist')

    # Validate the path is readable
    if os.access(thePath, os.R_OK):
        return thePath
    else:
        raise argparse.ArgumentTypeError('Path is not readable')

#End ValidatePath

''' Specify and Parse the command line, validate the arguments
and return results'''

parser = argparse.ArgumentParser('File System Baseline Creator
with PowerShell- Version 1.0 December 2018')

parser.add_argument('-b', '--baseline',
required=True,
help="Specify the resulting dictionary baseline file")

parser.add_argument('-p', '--Path',
required=True, type= ValidatePath,
help="Specify the target folder to baseline")

parser.add_argument('-t', '--tmp',
required=True,
help="Specify a temporary result file for the PowerShell Script")
```

```python
args = parser.parse_args()

baselineFile = args.baseline
targetPath   = args.Path
tmpFile      = args.tmp

''' MAIN SCRIPT SECTION '''
if __name__ == '__main__':

    try:
        ''' POWERSHELL EXECUTION SECTION '''
        command = "powershell -ExecutionPolicy ByPass
-File C:/PS/HashAcquire.ps1"+"
-TargetFolder "+ targetPath+" -ResultFile "+ tmpFile

        print(command)

        powerShellResult = subprocess.run(command,
        stdout=subprocess.PIPE)

        if powerShellResult.stderr == None:

            ''' DICTIONARY CREATION SECTION '''
            baseDict = {}

            with open(tmpFile, 'r') as inFile:
                for eachLine in inFile:
                    lineList = eachLine.split()
                    if len(lineList) == 2:
                        hashValue = lineList[0]
                        fileName  = lineList[1]
                        baseDict[hashValue] = fileName
                    else:
                        continue
```

```
        with open(baselineFile, 'wb') as outFile:
            pickle.dump(baseDict, outFile)

        print("Baseline: ", baselineFile,
" Created with:", "{:,}".format(len(baseDict)), "Records")
            print("Script Terminated Successfully")
    else:
        print("PowerShell Error:", p.stderr)

  except Exception as err:
      print ("Cannot Create Output File: "+str(err))
      quit()
```

Those new to Python might find this script a bit complicated. Therefore, the script has been broken down into the following sections here:

1. LIBRARY IMPORT

2. ARGUMENT PARSING

3. MAIN

4. POWERSHELL EXECUTION

5. DICTIONARY CREATION

LIBRARY IMPORT: As the name implies, this is where the needed Python libraries are loaded. They include:

- subprocess: Used to launch the PowerShell script

- os: Used for file and folder validation

- argparse: Used for parsing the command line arguments

- pickle: Used to store the resulting dictionary to a file for later use

ARGUMENT PARSING: This section sets up and then processes user command line arguments. For this script, the required arguments include the following:

- -b specifies the resulting dictionary baseline filename.

- -p specifies the target path to be used by the PowerShell script to store the extracted hash and filenames.

- -t specifies the tmp file that will be used by the PowerShell script to store the hash data.

The argparse library in Python automatically processes the command line and validates that the user has entered all the required arguments and will provide help if requested. Figure 4-9 depicts the test folder and the result of executing the script with only the -h option.

```
Administrator: Command Prompt                                          —  □  ×

C:\PS>dir
 Volume in drive C is OS
 Volume Serial Number is ECD2-7A54

 Directory of C:\PS

12/31/2018  10:53 AM    <DIR>          .
12/31/2018  10:53 AM    <DIR>          ..
12/31/2018  10:44 AM             2,712 CreateBaseline.py
12/10/2018  10:29 AM             2,820 EventProcessorFinal.ps1
12/29/2018  11:38 AM               979 HashAcquire.ps1
12/11/2018  10:43 AM               817 USBAcquire.ps1
               4 File(s)          7,328 bytes
               2 Dir(s)  171,765,731,328 bytes free

C:\PS>python CreateBaseline.py -h
usage: File System Baseline Creator with PowerShell- Version 1.0 December 2018
       [-h] -b BASELINE -p PATH -t TMP

optional arguments:
  -h, --help            show this help message and exit
  -b BASELINE, --baseline BASELINE
                        Specify the resulting baseline file
  -p PATH, --Path PATH  Specify the target folder to baseline
  -t TMP, --tmp TMP     Specify a temporary result file for the PowerShell
                        Script

C:\PS>
```

Figure 4-9. *Execution of the CreateBaseline.py script requesting help*

The argument processing section results in the creation of three variables:

1. [-b] baselineFile: Which specifies the resulting baseline dictionary file. This file will be created by the Python script.

2. [-p] targetPath: Which is passed to the PowerShell script to specify which folder to baseline. This is used by the PowerShell script.

3. [-t] tmpFile: Which is passed to the PowerShell script to specify the resulting temporary text file that will hold the intermediate results. The Python script uses this temporary file once generated by the PowerShell script.

MAIN: The main section performs the core elements of the script once the preliminary setup is complete.

POWERSHELL EXECUTION: This section launches the PowerShell script. It first creates a variable named **command** that will be used by the subprocess.run() method to launch the PowerShell script. Note that the execution in this case specifies a file, -File vs. a command, -Command that was used in the previous examples. It specifies the PowerShell script HashAcquire.ps1. Upon completion of the subprocess command, the standard error or stderr result is checked for successful completion. The result should be None. If not, the Python script will report the error returned.

DICTIONARY CREATION: If the PowerShell command was completed successfully, the temporary result file is then processed by the Python script in order to create the dictionary. Since the format of the resulting file is defined in the PowerShell script, processing each line of the file to extract the hash value and file path can be accomplished using a Python iteration loop. A dictionary entry is created for each line using the Hash

Value as the **Key** and the File Path as the **Value** of the KEY/VALUE pair. Once all the lines have been processed, the Python pickle library is used to store the created dictionary in the file specified on the command line which is now contained in the variable baselineFile. The Python script will then report details of the script. If any errors or exceptions occur during the Python script, the script will report the exception.

Figure 4-10 shows a successful execution of the CreateBaseline.py Python combined with the HashAcquire.ps1 PowerShell script. As you can see, the script produced 447 dictionary entries for the files contained in the c:/windows/system32/drivers/ folder. In addition, the two specified files baseline.txt and baseline.pickle were created in the c:/PS/ folder.

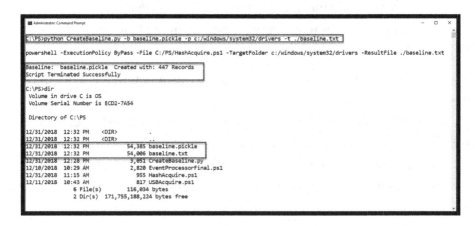

Figure 4-10. *Python/PowerShell script combined script execution*

Verifying the Baseline with Python

The next step is to create a Python Script that will verify that the current version of the selected folder has not changed. Basically, we are creating a simple tripwire of sorts. What are the specific validations that should be accomplished by the verification script?

1. Have any files been added?

2. Have any files been deleted?

3. Have any files been changed?

We are going to reuse the HashAcquire.ps1 PowerShell script and make some modifications to the processing of each entry returned by HashAcquire.ps1. For the most part, the VerifyBaseline.py script looks almost identical to the CreateBaseline.py script. The only modifications include:

1. Addition of the BASELINE DICTIONARY LOAD SECTION

2. Addition of the DICTIONARY TEST SECTION and associated dictionary validation functions

Listing 4-4 contains the full verification Python script. Note the HashAcquire.ps1 PowerShell script is unchanged.

Listing 4-4. Verify Baseline Python Script

```
'''

Step Two Verify a baseline hash list against a target folder
December 2018, Python Forensics

'''

''' LIBRARY IMPORT SECTION '''

import subprocess        # subprocess library
import argparse          # argument parsing library
import os                # Operating System Path
import pickle            # Python object serialization

"'ARGUMENT PARSING SECTION "'
```

```python
def ValidatePath(thePath):
    ''' Validate the Folder thePath
        it must exist and we must have rights
        to read from the folder.
        raise the appropriate error if either
        is not true
    '''

    # Validate the path exists
    if not os.path.exists(thePath):
        raise argparse.ArgumentTypeError('Path does not exist')

    # Validate the path is readable
    if os.access(thePath, os.R_OK):
        return thePath
    else:
        raise argparse.ArgumentTypeError('Path is not readable')

#End ValidatePath ====================================

''' Specify and Parse the command line, validate the arguments
and return results'''

parser = argparse.ArgumentParser('File System Baseline
Validation with PowerShell- Version 1.0 December 2018')

parser.add_argument('-b', '--baseline',required=True,
help="Specify the source baseline file to verify")

parser.add_argument('-p', '--Path',
type= ValidatePath, required=True,
help="Specify the target folder to verify")

parser.add_argument('-t', '--tmp', required=True,
help="Specify a temporary result file for the PowerShell Script")
```

```python
args = parser.parse_args()

baselineFile = args.baseline
targetPath   = args.Path
tmpFile      = args.tmp

def TestDictEquality(d1,d2):
    """ return True if all keys and values are the same
        otherwise return False """
    if all(k in d2 and d1[k] == d2[k] for k in d1):
        if all(k in d1 and d1[k] == d2[k] for k in d2):
            return True
        else:
            return False
    else:
        return False

    '''

    return all(k in d2 and d1[k] == d2[k]
               for k in d1) \
        and all(k in d1 and d1[k] == d2[k]
               for k in d2)
    '''

def TestDictDiff(d1, d2):
    """ return the subset of d1 where the keys don't exist in
    d2 or the values in d2 are different, as adict """
    diff = {}

    for k,v in d1.items():
        if k in d2 and v in d2[k]:
            continue
```

```
        else:
            diff[k+v] = "Baseline Missmatch"

    return diff

''' MAIN SCRIPT SECTION '''
if __name__ == '__main__':

    try:
        ''' POWERSHELL EXECUTION SECTION '''
        print()
        command = "powershell -ExecutionPolicy ByPass -File
        C:/PS/HashAcquire.ps1"+" -TargetFolder "+ targetPath+"
        -ResultFile "+ tmpFile
        print(command)
        print()

        powerShellResult = subprocess.run(command,
        stdout=subprocess.PIPE)
        if powerShellResult.stderr == None:

            ''' BASELINE DICTIONARY LOAD SECTION '''
            # Load in the baseline dictionary

            with open(baselineFile, 'rb') as baseIn:
                baseDict = pickle.load(baseIn)

            ''' DICTIONARY CREATION SECTION '''

            # Create a new dictionary for the target folder
            newDict  = {}

            with open(tmpFile, 'r') as inFile:
                for eachLine in inFile:
                    lineList = eachLine.split()
```

```
            if len(lineList) == 2:
                hashValue = lineList[0]
                fileName  = lineList[1]
                newDict[hashValue] = fileName
            else:
                continue

        ''' DICTIONARY TEST SECTION '''
        if TestDictEquality(baseDict, newDict):
            print("No Changes Detected")
        else:
            diff = TestDictDiff(newDict, baseDict)
            print(diff)

    else:
        print("PowerShell Error:", p.stderr)

except Exception as err:
    print ("Cannot Create Output File: "+str(err))
    quit()
```

Overview of the New Code Sections in VerifyBaseline.py

DICTIONARY LOAD: This section loads the specified dictionary from the saved pickle file that was created in the CreateBaseline.py script. The pickle. load() method is used to restore the dictionary from the specified file.

DICTIONARY TEST: This section utilizes two newly created functions:

- TestDictEquality()

- TestDictDiff()

The TestDictEquality function compares the newly created dictionary of the target folder with the saved dictionary that was loaded using the pickle.load() method. The two dictionaries

- baseDict

- newDict

contain the dictionaries to compare. The dictionaries contain the SHA-256 Hash (key) and Filename (Value) for each dictionary. Python provides many useful built-in mechanisms to compare and iterate through dictionaries. The TestDictEquality function verifies that the two dictionaries are an exact match. And if they are, True is returned by the function. If they are not equivalent, then the function returns False. To determine what discrepancies exist, the TestDictDiff() function is called only when inequality exists.

The TestDictDiff function compares the contents of the baseDict with the newDict and creates a new dictionary to hold any mismatching values. The dictionary containing any differences is returned by the TestDictDiff function. Once returned, the contents of the diffDictionary are displayed.

Figure 4-11 displays the execution of the VerifyBaseline.py script including the new help results and no changes detected.

```
Administrator: Command Prompt                                                    —  □  ×

C:\PS>python VerifyBaseline.py -h
usage: File System Baseline Validation with PowerShell- Version 1.0 December 2018
       [-h] -b BASELINE -p PATH -t TMP

optional arguments:
  -h, --help            show this help message and exit
  -b BASELINE, --baseline BASELINE
                        Specify the source baseline file to verify
  -p PATH, --Path PATH  Specify the target folder to verify
  -t TMP, --tmp TMP     Specify a temporary result file for the PowerShell
                        Script

C:\PS>python VerifyBaseline.py -b baseline.pickle -p c:/windows/system32/drivers/ -t c:/PS/tmp.txt

powershell -ExecutionPolicy ByPass -File C:/PS/HashAcquire.ps1 -TargetFolder c:/windows/system32/drivers/ -ResultFile c:/PS/tmp.txt

No Changes Detected

C:\PS>_
```

Figure 4-11. *Verify baseline execution and help with no changes*

Figure 4-12 shows the execution of the VerifyBaseline.py script which identifies two innocuous files added to the c:/windows/system32/drivers directory.

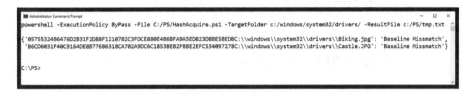

Figure 4-12. *Verify baseline execution with detected changes*

Overview of Python Execution with PowerShell

This example provides a nice model for the execution and post-processing of PowerShell results from Python. More importantly, this model can be extended for several other uses. For example:

1. By modifying the PowerShell script and parameters, the target ComputerName could be added. The PowerShell Script could next add the Invoke-Command CmdLet and then perform remote acquisitions, something that would be much more difficult to do from Python only. Thus, we're using PowerShell as the acquisition engine and Python as the backed processor. Here is an example of the modified PowerShell Command that would be necessary:

```
Invoke-Command -ComputerName $targetComputer
-Credential $User
-ScriptBlock {Get-ChildItem $TargetFolder |
Get-FileHash | Select-Object -Property Hash,
Path | Format-Table -HideTableHeaders | Out-File
$ResultFile -Encoding ascii}
```

117

2. The acquisition CmdLet Get-ChildItem could be replaced with a plethora of other acquisition-oriented CmdLets such as:

- Get-Process

- Get-Service

- Get-NetTCPConnections

- Get-NetFirewallSetting

- Or any other local or network values of investigative interest

Then, without modification the Python CreateBaseline and VerifyBaseline scripts can be applied to create baselines and then detect any changes across your environment.

3. The interface model using subprocess.run() can be applied to other acquisitions of PowerShell scripts. Using the model of creating simple ASCII result files that can be ingested line by line from Python, establish a solid interface between Python and PowerShell. You could of course return the data via standard out. However, this method is less stable when generating significant output from PowerShell.

Challenge Problem: Perform Remote Script Execution

Utilizing what you have learned about the execution of PowerShell scripts from Python and the model that has been provided:

1. Expand upon the solution provided by exploring other PowerShell CmdLets that provide investigative or incident response value. Adjust the PowerShell and Python scripts as required.

    a. Get-Process

    b. Get-Service

    c. Get-NETTCPConnections

    d. Get-FirewallSettings

2. Modify the PowerShell and Python scripts to include access to other computers. This will require changes to both scripts in order to provide the name(s) of the additional computer. In addition, the PowerShell script will need to add the appropriate Invoke-Command CmdLet.

Summary

This chapter focused on the execution of PowerShell CmdLets and scripts directed via Python. The chapter covered the key method for interfacing with PowerShell using the Python subprocess library.

In addition, methods for delivering PowerShell results to Python for post-processing were discussed. A reusable model for this integration delivers a baseline for the integration of PowerShell and Python.

Finally, the Python language, libraries, and data types were discussed by example. These included argument parsing, subprocess usage, dictionaries, functions, and the general Python program structure.

Chapter 5 will expand on PowerShell and Python integration with additional examples and methods.

CHAPTER 5

PowerShell/Python Investigation Example

The ability to gather remote activities during incident response situations is one of the key strengths of PowerShell. The infrastructure provided with the latest version of PowerShell significantly reduces the network setup required and offers significant security.

Integrating PowerShell and Python provides a viable platform for local and remote investigations. The "old" way of connecting to machines remotely is by using DCOM (Distributed Component Object Model) and/or RPCs (Remote Procedure Calls). These methods of integration involve significant complexities, and in some cases vulnerabilities, based upon the number of ports that need configuration.

The new method is called PowerShell Remoting. Remember, we saw the basics of this in Chapter 3, using the Invoke-Command CmdLet. In this chapter, we will take a much deeper look at PowerShell Remoting. However, before using the new PowerShell Remoting capability, it may need to be enabled in your environment. One of the nice features of PowerShell Remoting is that it runs over HTTPS, and it is done over a single port – port 5985.

© Chet Hosmer 2019
C. Hosmer, *PowerShell and Python Together*, https://doi.org/10.1007/978-1-4842-4504-0_5

Enable PowerShell Remoting

The first step is to enable PowerShell Remoting on your investigative machine (the one you are performing the investigation from). You probably already guessed that we are going to do this with a PowerShell CmdLet. Interestingly enough, this one is titled Enable-PSRemoting. As always, you start with Get-Help in order to understand the parameters and options (Listing 5-1).

Listing 5-1. Get-Help Enable-PSRemoting

```
PS C:\PS> Get-Help Enable-PSRemoting

NAME
    Enable-PSRemoting

SYNOPSIS
    Configures the computer to receive remote commands.

SYNTAX
    Enable-PSRemoting [-Confirm] [-Force]
    [-SkipNetworkProfileCheck] [-WhatIf] [<CommonParameters>]

DESCRIPTION
    The Enable-PSRemoting cmdlet configures the computer to
    receive Windows PowerShell remote commands that are sent by
    using the WS-Management technology.

    By default, on Windows Server® 2012, Windows PowerShell
    remoting is enabled. You can use Enable-PSRemoting to
    enable Windows PowerShell remoting on other supported
    versions of Windows and to re-enable remoting on Windows
    Server 2012 if it becomes disabled.
```

You have to run this command only one time on each computer that will receive commands. You do not have to run it on computers that only send commands. Because the configuration starts listeners, it is prudent to run it only where it is needed.

Beginning in Windows PowerShell 3.0, the Enable-PSRemoting cmdlet can enable Windows PowerShell remoting on client versions of Windows when the computer is on a public network.
For more information, see the description of the SkipNetworkProfileCheck parameter.

The Enable-PSRemoting cmdlet performs the following operations:

- Runs the Set-WSManQuickConfighttp://go.microsoft. com/fwlink/?LinkID=141463 cmdlet, which performs the following tasks:

----- Starts the WinRM service.

----- Sets the startup type on the WinRM service to Automatic.

----- Creates a listener to accept requests on any IP address, if one does not already exist.

----- Enables a firewall exception for WS-Management communications.

----- Registers the Microsoft.PowerShell and Microsoft. PowerShell.Workflow session configurations, if it they are not already registered.

----- Registers the Microsoft.PowerShell32 session
        configuration on 64-bit computers, if it is not
        already registered.

----- Enables all session configurations.

----- Changes the security descriptor of all session
        configurations to allow remote access.

----- Restarts the WinRM service to make the preceding
        changes effective.

To run this cmdlet, start Windows PowerShell by using the
Run as administrator option.
CAUTION: On systems that have both Windows PowerShell 3.0
and Windows PowerShell 2.0, do not use Windows PowerShell
2.0 to run the Enable-PSRemoting and Disable-PSRemoting
cmdlets. The commands might appear to succeed, but the
remoting is not configured correctly. Remote commands and
later attempts to enable and disable remoting, are likely
to fail.

RELATED LINKS
    Online Version: http://go.microsoft.com/fwlink/?LinkId=821475
    Disable-PSSessionConfiguration
    Enable-PSSessionConfiguration
    Get-PSSessionConfiguration
    Register-PSSessionConfiguration
    Set-PSSessionConfiguration
    Disable-PSRemoting

REMARKS

To see the examples, type: "get-help Enable-PSRemoting
-examples".

For more information, type: "get-help Enable-PSRemoting
-detailed".

For technical information, type: "get-help Enable-
PSRemoting -full".

For online help, type: "get-help Enable-PSRemoting -online"

When executing PSRemoting, use the -Force option to eliminate the
need for user confirmation throughout the process. Figure 5-1 depicts the
CmdLet execution.

Note   Since this is already enabled on the local machine, it provides
the following feedback. Windows Remote Management (WinRM)
is likely to be required when Enabling PSRemoting. Each system,
network, and OS configuration is different, so consult your system
administrator for assistance. Microsoft and third parties provide
information on proper setup. Please consult these guides for more
information. Also, this setup needs to be done on the computers that
you wish to investigate as well.

https://docs.microsoft.com/en-us/powershell/module/
microsoft.powershell.core/enable-psremoting?view=pow
ershell-6

https://docs.microsoft.com/en-us/windows/desktop/
winrm/winrm-powershell-commandlets

www.howtogeek.com/117192/how-to-run-powershell-
commands-on-remote-computers/

```
PS C:\PS> Enable-PSRemoting -Force
WinRM is already set up to receive requests on this computer.
WinRM is already set up for remote management on this computer.

PS C:\PS>
```

Figure 5-1. *Enable PowerShell Remoting*

Note   One final note regarding the enabling of PowerShell Remoting. The network configuration for all of your adapters must be set to Private not Public for security reasons. Please again contact your system administrator to make these changes, as parameters depend upon the operating system and version you are using.

Gathering and Analyzing Remote Evidence

Utilizing a combination of PowerShell and Python to gather evidence from systems other than the one we are running on is critical in order to expand the scope of our investigations. Let's first look at a very useful PowerShell CmdLet for both local and remote investigations: Get-DNSClientCache.

DNS Client cache, or DNS *resolver* cache, is a local database maintained by the operating system. It contains evidence of recent visits to web sites and other Internet locations. Simply put, DNS Client cache is just a record of recent DNS lookups that speeds access to already resolved web site IP addresses. Note that clearing the history of your web browser to hide your activity does not include the Operating Systems DNS resolver cache. Many cleaning programs will clear this cache, but it can be overlooked by users and it may provide important evidence of recent activity.

The DNS, or Doman Name System, provides a translation from friendly names like microsoft.com, google.com, and python-forensic.org to the IP addresses they reside at. Each time you enter an address in your browser like `www.amazon.com`, a DNS lookup is performed to translate the human readable address into an IP address that can be accessed.

Starting the Get DNSClientCache process after clearing the cache produces the following results.

```
PS C:\WINDOWS\system32> Get-DnsClientCache | Select-Object
-Property Entry
```

Of course, nothing is returned from the CmdLet because the cache is empty.

In order to add data to the DnsClientCache open a web browser and load the Google home page as shown in Figure 5-2.

Figure 5-2. *Launch browser and navigate to the Google home page*

Executing the CmdLet now delivers some expected and not-expected results (Listing 5-2).

Listing 5-2. Results from the Get-DnsClientCache CmdLet

```
PS C:\WINDOWS\system32> Get-DnsClientCache | Select-Object
-Property Entry

Entry
-----
beacons.gcp.gvt2.com
beacons.gcp.gvt2.com
beacons.gcp.gvt2.com
google.com
google.com
google.com
google.com
google.com
google.com
bolt.dropbox.com
```

The stored DNS locations for google.com would of course be expected since the google.com page was opened. However, what is the beacons.gcp.gvt.com lookup? It is owned by google according to online research and is used by google to track activity and to provide automated assist when you type in the Google search window. The bolt.dropbox.com is unrelated to the www.google.com access, rather it was accessed due to a routine sync as Dropbox is running on the system.

As with other CmdLets, Get-ClientDnsCache has additional properties and member functions associated with it. They can be examined by piping the output of Get-ClientDnsCache to Get-Member as shown in Figure 5-3.

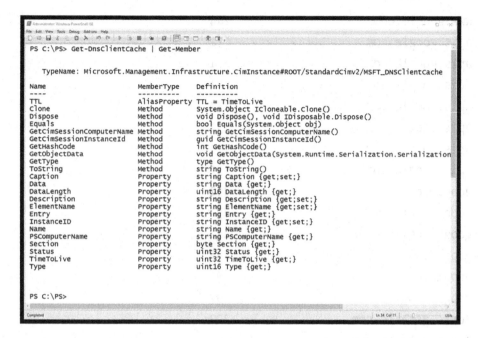

Figure 5-3. *Member methods and properties for Get-DnsClientCache*

One good example is the TimeToLive property, which provides information regarding how long the DNS Client cache entry will persist in seconds. The knowledge that these entries only exist for a specific period certainly requires some urgency in collecting this information during an investigation. See Listing 5-3.

Listing 5-3. Obtaining the Time to Live for Each DnsClientCache Entry

```
PS C:\WINDOWS\system32> Get-DnsClientCache | Select-Object
-Property Entry, TimetoLive

Entry                         TimetoLive
-----                         ----------

www.gstatic.com                       17
ssl.gstatic.com                      292
```

www.google.com	244
apis.google.com	131
apis.google.com	131
apis.google.com	131
apis.google.com	131
apis.google.com	131
apis.google.com	131
apis.google.com	131
google.com	292
google.com	292
google.com	292
google.com	292
google.com	292
google.com	292
fonts.gstatic.com	292
fonts.gstatic.com	292
encrypted-tbn0.gstatic.com	292

Invoking Remote Access

A more significant application of Get-DnsClientCache is of course to
execute this CmdLet remotely targeting systems under investigation.
Using the Invoke-Command, targeting of the Lenovo-Upstairs computer in
order to capture the recent DnsClientCaches is shown in Listing 5-4.
The output was abbreviated in order to highlight more interesting
locations, specifically the access to dfinews.com, forensicsmag.com, and
steganography.com.

Listing 5-4. Remote Invocation of Get-DnsClientCache

```
PS C:\WINDOWS\system32> Invoke-Command -ComputerName Lenovo-
Upstairs -Credential Lenovo-Upstairs\Remote-Admin -ScriptBlock
{Get-DnsClientCache | Select-Object -Property Entry |Out-String}

Entry
-----

www.dfinews.com
www.dfinews.com
www.forensicmag.com
www.forensicmag.com
www.forensicmag.com
www.forensicmag.com
www.forensicmag.com

...
... reduced results for brevity
...

steganography.com
steganography.com
www.wired.com
www.wired.com
www.wired.com
www.wired.com
```

Building a PowerShell Script for DnsCache Acquisition

Unfortunately, there were hundreds of cached entries to sort through when this CmdLet was launched. Filtering or searching these results would be a tedious process for investigators. Therefore, why not create a Python script that leverages a PowerShell script to search the results based on a list of suspicious web sites or keywords of interest? Using the PowerShell script model that was created in Chapter 4, only a few simple tweaks are necessary to have application here:

1. Change the synopsis

2. Change the description

3. Modify the input parameters

4. Utilize the Get-ClientDnsCache CmdLet

Listing 5-5 shows the PowerShell script.

Listing 5-5. CacheAcquire.ps1 PowerShell Script

```
<#
.synopsis
Collect ClientDnsCache

- User Specifies the target computer

The script will produce a simple ascii output file containing
the recent DnsCache from the target computer

.Description
This script collects DnsCache from the Target Computer

.parameter targetComputer
Specifies the computer to collect the USB Activity

.parameter user
Specifies the Administrator UserName on the Target Computer

.parameter resultFile
Specifies the full path of the output file
```

```
.example

./CacheAcquire.ps1 -user Lenovo-Upstairs\Remote-Admin
-targetComputer Lenovo-Upstairs -resultFile cache.txt

Collects the recent DnsCache from the target computer
#>

# Parameter Definition Section
param(
    [string]$user,
    [string]$targetComputer,
    [string]$resultFile
)

# Obtain the ClientDnsCache from target computer and store the
result in a local variable
$r = Invoke-Command -ComputerName $targetComputer -Credential
$user -ScriptBlock {Get-DnsClientCache | Select-Object
-Property Entry | Out-String}

# Write the resulting list in simple ascii to a specified
local file
$r | Out-File $resultFile -Encoding ascii
```

One important note: When using the Invoke-Command, any output file creation takes place on the remote system. Therefore, capture the result of the script in a variable ($r in this example) and then pipe the variable to the requested local file.

Sample execution of the script from within PowerShell ISE is shown in Figures 5-4 to 5-6.

Figure 5-4. *CacheAcquire.ps1 execution and credential entry*

Figure 5-5. *Resulting cache list*

Figure 5-6. *Resulting cache.txt file*

As with previous PowerShell scripts, using Get-Help will provide the details necessary to allow other users to also leverage the script (Listing 5-6).

Listing 5-6. Display Help for the CacheAcquire PowerShell Script

```
PS C:\PS> Get-Help .\CacheAcquire.ps1
NAME
    C:\PS\CacheAcquire.ps1

SYNOPSIS
    Collect ClientDnsCache

    - User Specifies the target computer

    The script will produce a simple ascii output file
    containing the recent DnsCache from the target computer

SYNTAX
    C:\PS\CacheAcquire.ps1 [[-user] <String>]
    [[-targetComputer] <String>] [[-resultFile] <String>]
    [<CommonParameters>]

DESCRIPTION
    This script collects DNS cache from the Target Computer

RELATED LINKS

REMARKS
    To see the examples, type: "get-help C:\PS\CacheAcquire.ps1
    -examples".
    For more information, type: "get-help C:\PS\CacheAcquire.
    ps1 -detailed".
    For technical information, type: "get-help C:\PS\
    CacheAcquire.ps1 -full".
```

Python Script and PowerShell CacheAquire Script

Now that we have a reliable PowerShell script to acquire DNS cache from remote computers, the next step is to build a Python script that will launch the PowerShell script, then search the subsequent results. The general concept is to search the acquired DNS cache using a set of keywords that are provided to the Python script from a file. See Listing 5-7.

Listing 5-7. AcquireDNS.py

```
'''

Acquire DNS Scripts from a Remote Computer
Version 1.0 January 2018
Author: Chet Hosmer
PYTHON Version 3.x is Required

'''

''' LIBRARY IMPORT SECTION '''

import subprocess        # subprocess library
import argparse          # argument parsing library
import os                # Operating System Path

''' ARGUMENT PARSING SECTION '''

def ValidateFile(theFile):
    ''' Validate the File exists
        it must exist and we must have rights
        to read from the folder.
        raise the appropriate error if either
        is not true
    '''
```

```
    # Validate the file exists
    if not os.path.exists(theFile):
        raise argparse.ArgumentTypeError('File does not exist')

    # Validate the file is readable
    if os.access(theFile, os.R_OK):
        return theFile
    else:
        raise argparse.ArgumentTypeError('File is not
        readable')

#End ValidateFile ====================================

''' Specify and Parse the command line, validate the arguments
and return results'''

parser = argparse.ArgumentParser('Remote Client DNS Cache with
PowerShell  - Version 1.0 January 2018')

parser.add_argument('-c', '--computer',  required=True,
                    help="Specify a target Computer for
                    Aquistion")

parser.add_argument('-u', '--user',      required=True,
                    help="Specify the remote user account")

parser.add_argument('-t', '--tmp',       required=True,
                    help="Specify a temporary result file for
                    the PowerShell Script")

parser.add_argument('-s', '--srch',      required=True,
                    type=ValidateFile, help="Specify the
                    keyword search file")
```

```python
args = parser.parse_args()

computer = args.computer
user     = args.user
tmp      = args.tmp
srch     = args.srch

print("DNS Cache Acquisition\n")

print("Target:        ", computer)
print("User:          ", user)
print("Keyword File: ", srch)

'''KEYWORD LOADING SECTION '''

print("Processing Keyword Input")
try:
    with open(srch, 'r') as keywordFile:
        words = keywordFile.read()
        word = words.lower()
        words = words.strip()
        wordList = words.split()
        wordSet = set(wordList)
        keyWordList = list(wordSet)
        print("\nKeywords to search")
        for eachKeyword in keyWordList:
            print(eachKeyword)
        print()
except Exception as err:
    print("Error Processing Keyword File: ", str(err))
    quit()
```

```python
''' MAIN SCRIPT SECTION '''
if __name__ == '__main__':

    try:
        "' POWERSHELL EXECUTION SECTION "'
        print()
        command = "powershell -ExecutionPolicy ByPass -File
        C:/PS/CacheAcquire.ps1"+" -targetComputer "+
        computer+ " -user "+user+ "
        -resultFile "+tmp

        print("Executing: ", command)
        print()

        powerShellResult = subprocess.run(command,
        stdout=subprocess.PIPE)

        if powerShellResult.stderr == None:

            '''DNS CACHE SEARCHING SECTION '''

            hitList = []
            try:
                with open(tmp, 'r') as results:
                    for eachLine in results:
                        eachLine = eachLine.strip()
                        eachLine = eachLine.lower()
                        for eachKeyword in keyWordList:
                            if eachKeyword in eachLine:
                                hitList.append(eachLine)
            except Exception as err:
                print("Error Processing Result File: ", str(err))
```

```
        '''RESULT OUTPUT SECTION '''

        print("Suspicous DNS Cache Entries Found")
        for eachEntry in hitList:
            print(eachEntry)

        print("\nScript Complete")
    else:
        print("PowerShell Error:", p.stderr)

except Exception as err:
    print ("Cannot Create Output File: "+str(err))
    quit()
```

The script has been broken down into the following sections. Each will be explained:

- LIBRARY IMPORT

- ARGUMENT PARSING

- KEYWORD LOADING

- POWERSHELL EXECUTION

- DNS CACHE SEARCHING

- RESULT OUTPUT

LIBRARY IMPORT: As the name implies, this is where the needed Python libraries are loaded. They include:

- subprocess: Used to launch the PowerShell script

- os: Used for file and folder validation

- argparse: Used for parsing the command line arguments

ARGUMENT PARSING: This section sets up and then processes user command line arguments. For this script the required arguments include the following:

- -c specifies the target computer name.

- -u specifies the remote computer user name.

- -t specifies the tmp file that will be used by the PowerShell script to store the acquired DNS cache data.

- -s specifies the local file that contains keywords to search.

The argparse library in Python automatically processes the command line and validates that the user has entered all the required arguments. The library will also provide help if requested. To obtain the help, simply execute the script with only the -h option as shown in Listing 5-8.

Listing 5-8. Python Script Help Output Using the -h Switch

```
usage: Remote Client DNS Cache with PowerShell- Version 1.0
January 2018
        [-h] -c COMPUTER -u USER -t TMP -s SRCH

optional arguments:
  -h, --help              show this help message and exit
  -c COMPUTER, --computer COMPUTER
                          Specify a target Computer for Aquistion
  -u USER, --user USER    Specify the remote user account
  -t TMP, --tmp TMP       Specify a temporary result file for the
                          PowerShell Script
  -s SRCH, --srch SRCH    Specify the keyword search file
```

KEYWORD LOADING: This section opens the designated keyword file and creates a list of unique keywords found in the file (Figure 5-7). The section strips any extraneous characters from each entry, and ensures that all entries are in lowercase to enable the best search matching.

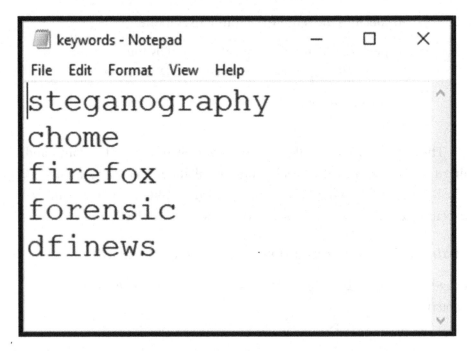

Figure 5-7. Sample keywords file

POWERSHELL EXECUTION: This section launches the PowerShell script. It first creates a variable named **command** that will be used by the subprocess.run() method to launch the PowerShell script. It specifies the PowerShell script CacheAcquire.ps1. Upon completion of the subprocess command, the standard error or stderr result is checked for successful completion. The result should be None. If not, the Python script will report the error generated by PowerShell.

DNS CACHE SEARCHING: This section processes each line from the cache results generated by PowerShell. Each line is then checked to determine if any of the unique keywordsv are found. If a keyword is detected, that entire line is stored in the Python *hitList* variable.

RESULT OUTPUT: This section iterates through each entry of the Python *hitList* variable and prints each result to the screen.

Figure 5-8 depicts the successful execution of the AcquireDNS.py Python script that leverages the CacheAcquire.ps1 PowerShell script. The script was executed from the Windows command line with administrator privilege.

```
C:\PS>python AcquireDNS.py -c PYTHON-3
-u PYTHON-3\USER-HIDDEN -t c:\ps\tmp.txt -s c:\ps\keywords.txt
```

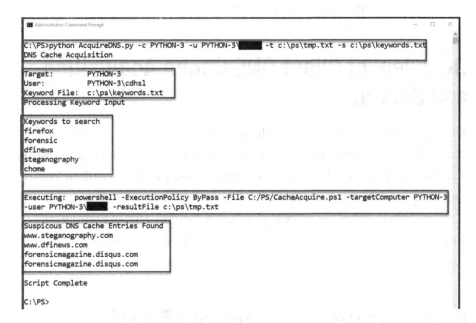

Figure 5-8. *Acquire DNS remote in action*

The script output first shows:

1. Details of the extracted command line arguments:

    a. Target Computer

    b. Remote User Name

    c. Local Keyword File

2. The decoded list of keywords that were extracted from the local keyword file

3. The details of the PowerShell command line generated from the inputs

4. The matching DNS cache entries that contain keywords from the keyword list

Overview of Client DNS Cache Acquisition and Search

This example expands on the model that leverages the PowerShell acquisition strengths with a Python script that can search the results. More importantly, this model was used to acquire Client DNS cache data from a specified remote computer using the Invoke-Command CmdLet.

The Python script could be expanded to include a list of computers and relevant user accounts in order to automate the acquisition and the automated search of Client DNS cache on demand.

Challenge Problem: Multiple Target Computer DNSCache Acquisition

Utilizing what you have learned about the execution of PowerShell scripts from Python and the model that has been provided:

- Expand upon the solution provided by loading a list of target computes along with the required user accounts.

- In addition to searching each of the resulting Client DNS cache results, determine which DNS entries were common across all the computers that were accessed.

Summary

This chapter focused on the execution of PowerShell CmdLets and scripts directed via Python to acquire Client DNS cache from both the local computer and a specified remote device. The chapter delivered yet another PowerShell script that can be used either standalone or driven by the accompanying Python script to access, process, and search the results.

Finally, the Python language, libraries, and data types were discussed by example. These included argument parsing, subprocess usage, dictionaries, functions, and the general Python program structure.

Chapter 6 will discuss some future considerations that can expand upon the combination of PowerShell and Python for investigative use. In addition, the included appendix provides both PowerShell and Python/ PowerShell combined examples that deliver a solid baseline for future investigations and expansion.

CHAPTER 6

Launching Python from PowerShell

So far, the approach to integrating Python with PowerShell has been to launch PowerShell scripts from Python as a subprocess. In this chapter, the roles will be reversed, and PowerShell will feed data to Python scripts. One of the key elements of PowerShell is pipelining the process of transferring the results of one CmdLet to the next. With that in mind, why not treat Python as just another pipeline element and execute Python scripts driven by data acquired by PowerShell?

Reversing Roles from PowerShell to Python

A PowerShell script and a Python script are both necessary to illustrate this method. We will start with a simple PowerShell script to pass a string of data across the pipe and display that data from the Python script.

© Chet Hosmer 2019
C. Hosmer, *PowerShell and Python Together*, https://doi.org/10.1007/978-1-4842-4504-0_6

Examine the PowerShell Script

Let's examine the details of the PowerShell script shown in Figure 6-1. The script is broken down into four simple steps:

1. Define a local variable $Python with the full path to the Python executable of your choice. For this example, Python 3.x will be again used.

2. Define a local variable $Script that defines the full path to the Python script that will be executed.

3. Define a local variable $Message that will be passed via the pipeline to the Python script.

4. This line passes the contents of the variable message to the Python script. The key element here is the ampersand (&) that directs PowerShell to launch the external program.

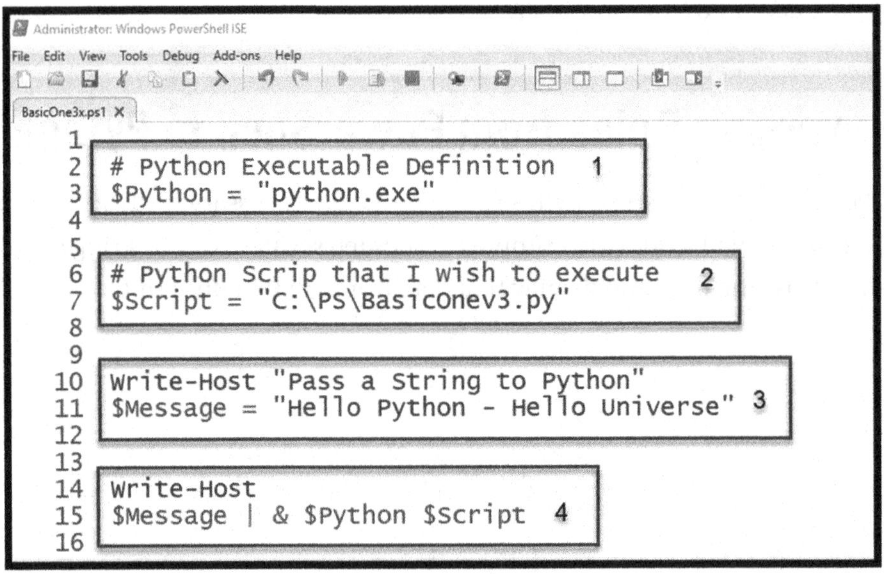

Figure 6-1. *BasicOne.ps1 PowerShell script*

Examine the Corresponding Python Script

Examining the corresponding Python script shown in Figure 6-2, we see that it is broken down into four sections as well:

1. A comment block that defines what the script will perform.

2. Import of the Python Standard Library sys. This is needed to process the data passed across the pipeline.

3. Print messages delivered from Python to demonstrate that the Python script is executing.

4. Processes each line delivered to the script via the pipeline and print the contents of each line. Note that in this example there is only one line passed.

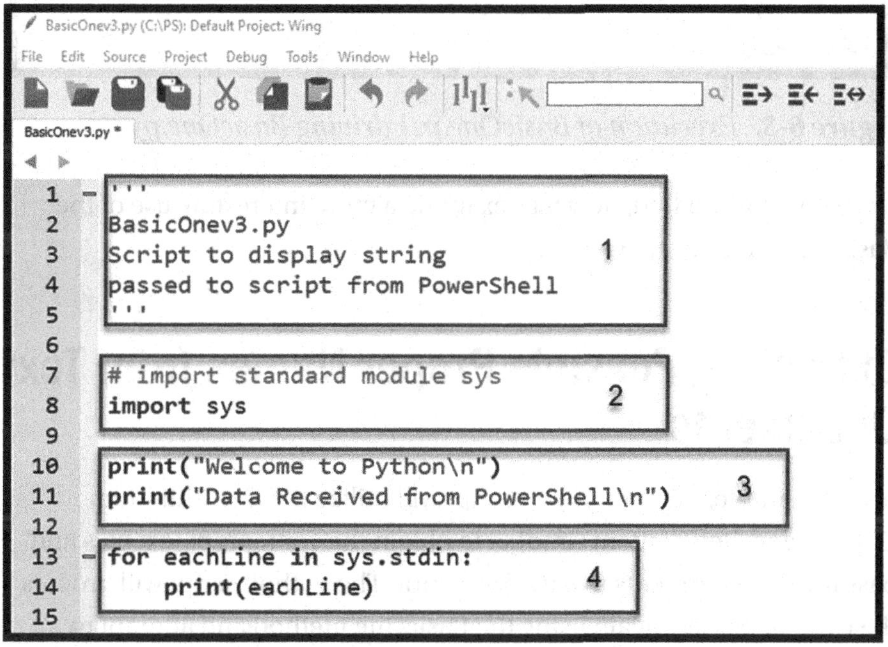

Figure 6-2. *BasicOne.py Python script*

Executing the Combined PowerShell to Python Scripts

Figure 6-3 depicts the resulting output generated by the PowerShell script driving the Python script. You'll notice that that the output from both the PowerShell script (write-host CmdLet) and the Python (print) statements appear in the PowerShell output.

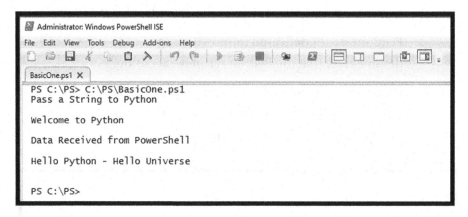

Figure 6-3. *Execution of BasicOne.ps1 driving BasicOne.py*

Using this method, now let's examine a more interesting use of the BasicOne method shown here.

Extracting Possible Proper Names from Text Documents

In this example, the PowerShell script will utilize the Get-ChildItem CmdLet and Get-Content CmdLet to obtain the contents of text files and pass the entire contents to a Python script. The Python script will process the content passed, again using the BasicOne method and attempt to extract possible proper names.

When examining simple text data during a forensic investigation, it is often useful to extract and rank proper names by the highest number of occurrences. The Python language has built-in capabilities that will perform this extraction swiftly and easily.

BUT FIRST, WHAT IS A PROPER NAME?

Linguistics defines proper names as those words that represent a person, place, group, organization, or thing that typically begins with a capital letter. For example, proper names in a single word (such as David, Smith, Carol, Washington, Canada, Pentagon, Congress, or Apple) can provide context and value to the investigation. In normal texts, these proper names are *most likely* capitalized and quite easy to strip, identify, count, and sort. It should be noted that not everyone would routinely capitalize proper names; however, smartphones, text messaging apps, e-mail programs, word processors, and even the Skype chat window automatically capitalize these for us. Thus, extracting and ranking them can provide a quick look and provide perspective to an investigation.

Examine the PowerShell Script

Figure 6-4 shows the PowerShell script that will deliver the content of these files to the more complex Python script that will perform the extraction and ranking of the possible proper names. Note, for this example, a new element has been added to allow the processing of multiple files.

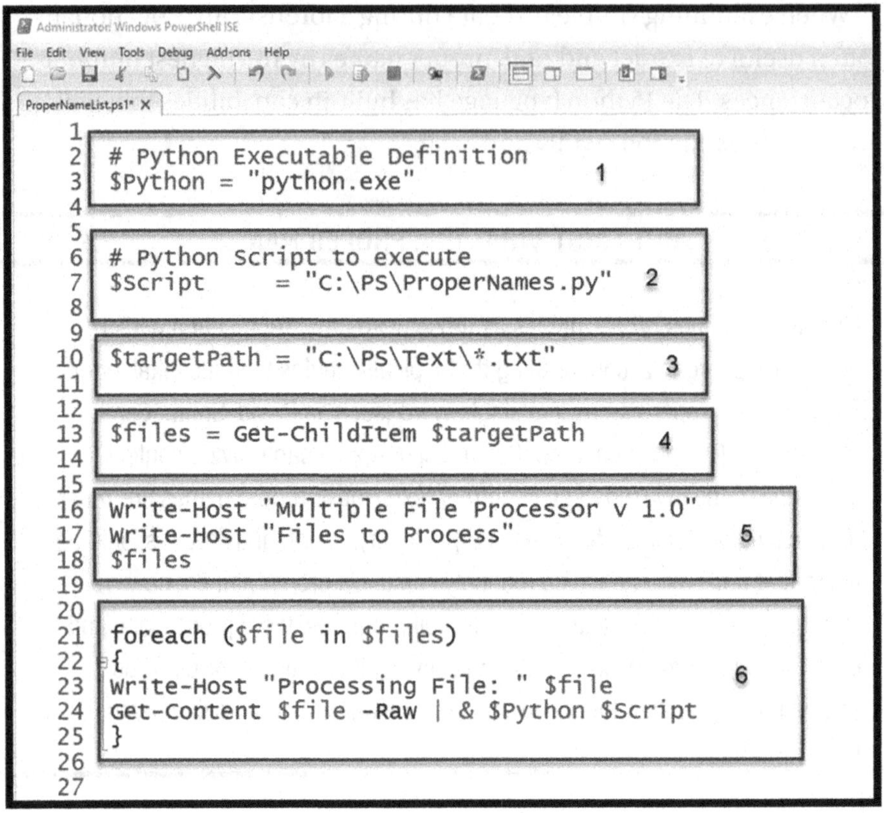

Figure 6-4. *PowerShell ProperNames script*

The script has been broken down into six steps. Each step is defined here:

1. Define a local variable $Python with the full path to the Python executable of your choice.

2. Define a local variable $Script that identifies the full path to the Python script that will be executed.

3. Define a local variable $targetPath that identifies the target path and file types to process.

4. Utilize the Get-ChildItem CmdLet to obtain the names of the files that match the extension provided.

5.   Write information to the host that includes the list of files that were discovered by the Get-ChildItem CmdLet.

6.   Using a ForEach loop, process each file listed in the local variable $files. Within the loop the script prints out the name of each file, then extracts the raw content of the file and pipes the resulting content to the Python script.

Examine the Corresponding Python ProperNames Script

The Python script shown in Listing 6-1 is broken down into six major sections described here:

1.   LIBRARY IMPORT

2.   STOP WORDS LIST DEFINITION

3.   DEFINING PSEUDO CONSTANTS

4.   EXTRACT PROPER NAMES

5.   MAIN PROGRAM ENTRY

6.   PRINT RESULTING POSSIBLE PROPER NAMES

LIBRARY IMPORT: As the name implies, this is where the needed Python libraries are loaded. They include:

- sys: As demonstrated in BasicOne, this library allows us to process command line input delivered by PowerShell.

- re: The Python regular expression library is used in this script to strip out extraneous character from the text in order to simplify the search for proper names.

- datetime: As the name implies, this library provides methods for display and calculating time and date details.

STOP WORDS LIST DEFINITION: This section creates a list of stop words that are used to within the script eliminate words that do not provide probative value when assessing proper names. They are in fact words that commonly start sentences that would be capitalized. Thus, eliminating these words from the results produces improved results.

DEFINING PSEUDO CONSTANTS: Traditional constants do not exist in the Python language, however, by capitalizing these variable alerts the reader that these variables should not be altered. In this case the variables MIN_SIZE and MAX_SIZE define the limits on possible proper names. By changing these values, you can widen or narrow the range of possible proper names.

EXTRACT PROPER NAMES FUNCTION: This is the core function of the script that processes the content piped from the PowerShell script. The function will be called for each line processed from standard input. The function extract possible proper names from the string input and add them to the dictionary. If the name already exists in the dictionary the function updates the dictionary value which contains the occurrences for that specific possible proper name.

MAIN PROGRAM ENTRY: The main program first prints several heading messages. Then creates an empty properNamesDictionary. Then as in the BasicOne.py example the script processes each line from the system standard input provided by the PowerShell script. Each line is then converted using the regular expression to eliminate any non-alpha characters. Each converted string is passed the ExtractProperNames function along with the current properNamesDictionary. This process is then repeated for each line provided to the script.

PRINT RESULTING POSSIBLE PROPER NAMES: The final section sorts the resulting dictionary by occurrences (highest first) and then prints out each proper name and the associated counts.

Listing 6-1. Python ProperNames.py Script

```
'''

Copyright (c) 2019 Python Forensics and Chet Hosmer

Permission is hereby granted, free of charge, to any person
obtaining a copy of this softwareand associated documentation
files (the "Software"), to deal in the Software without
restriction, including without limitation the rights to use, copy,
modify, merge, publish, distribute, sublicense, and/or sell copies
of the Software, and to permit persons to whom the Software is
furnished to do so, subject to the following conditions:

The above copyright notice and this permission notice shall be
included in all copies or substantial
portions of the Software.

 ProperNames Demonstration
 Version 1.3
 January 2019

 Requirement: Python 3.x

 usage:
 stdin | python properNames.py

 Script will process the piped data

'''

''' LIBRARY IMPORT SECTION '''

# import standard module sys
import sys

# import the regular expression library
# in order to filter out unwanted characters
import re
```

```python
# import datetime method from Standard Library
from datetime import datetime

''' STOP WORDS LIST DEFINITION SECTION '''

# COMMON STOP WORDS LIST
# What are stop_words: Words which are
# typically filtered
# out when processing natural language data (text)
# feel free to add additional words to the list

STOP_WORDS = [
"able","about","above","accordance","according",
"accordingly","across","actually","added","affected",
"affecting","affects","after","afterwards","again",
"against","almost","alone","along","already","also",
"although","always","among","amongst","announce",
"another","anybody","anyhow","anymore","anyone",
"anything","anyway","anyways","anywhere","apparently",
"approximately","arent","arise","around","aside",
"asking","auth","available","away","awfully","back",
"became","because","become","becomes","becoming",
"been","before","beforehand","begin","beginning",
"beginnings","begins","behind","being",
"believe","below","beside","besides","between",
"beyond","both","brief","briefly","came","cannot",
"cause","causes","certain","certainly","come",
"comes","contain","containing","contains","could",
"couldnt","date","different","does","doing","done",
"down","downwards","during","each","effect","eight",
"eighty","either","else","elsewhere","end",
"ending","enough","especially","even","ever",
"every","everybody","everyone","everything",
```

"everywhere","except","fifth","first","five",
"followed","following","follows","former","formerly",
"forth","found","four","from","further",
"furthermore","gave","gets","getting",
"give","given","gives","giving","goes",
"gone","gotten","happens","hardly","has","have",
"having","hence","here","hereafter","hereby",
"herein","heres","hereupon","hers","herself",
"himself","hither","home","howbeit","however",
"hundred","immediate","immediately","importance",
"important","indeed","index","information",
"instead","into","invention","inward","itself",
"just","keep","keeps","kept","know","known",
"knows","largely","last","lately","later","latter",
"latterly","least","less","lest","lets","like",
"liked","likely","line","little","look","looking",
"looks","made","mainly","make","makes","many",
"maybe","mean","means","meantime","meanwhile",
"merely","might","million","miss","more","moreover",
"most","mostly","much","must","myself","name",
"namely","near","nearly","necessarily","necessary",
"need","needs","neither","never","nevertheless",
"next","nine","ninety","nobody","none","nonetheless",
"noone","normally","noted","nothing","nowhere",
"obtain","obtained","obviously","often","okay",
"omitted","once","ones","only","onto","other",
"others","otherwise","ought","ours","ourselves",
"outside","over","overall","owing","page","pages",
"part","particular","particularly","past","perhaps",
"placed","please","plus","poorly","possible","possibly",
"potentially","predominantly","present","previously",
"primarily","probably","promptly","proud","provides",

"quickly","quite","rather","readily","really","recent",
"recently","refs","regarding","regardless",
"regards","related","relatively","research",
"respectively","resulted","resulting","results","right",
"run","said","same","saying","says","section","see",
"seeing","seem","seemed","seeming","seems","seen",
"self","selves","sent","seven","several","shall",
"shed","shes","should","show","showed","shown",
"showns","shows","significant","significantly",
"similar","similarly","since","slightly","some",
"somebody","somehow","someone","somethan",
"something","sometime","sometimes","somewhat",
"somewhere","soon","sorry","specifically","specified",
"specify","specifying","still","stop","strongly",
"substantially","successfully","such","sufficiently",
"suggest","sure","take","taken","taking","tell",
"tends","than","thank","thanks","thanx","that",
"thats","their","theirs","them","themselves","then",
"thence","there","thereafter","thereby","thered",
"therefore","therein","thereof","therere",
"theres","thereto","thereupon","there've","these",
"they","think","this","those","thou","though","thought",
"thousand","through","throughout","thru","thus",
"together","took","toward","towards","tried","tries",
"truly","trying","twice","under","unfortunately",
"unless","unlike","unlikely","until","unto","upon",
"used","useful","usefully","usefulness","uses","using",
"usually","value","various","very","want","wants",
"was","wasnt","welcome","went","were","what","whatever",
"when","whence","whenever","where","whereafter","whereas",
"whereby","wherein","wheres","whereupon","wherever",
"whether","which","while","whim","whither","whod",

```
"whoever","whole","whom","whomever","whos","whose",
"widely","will","willing","wish","with","within","without",
"wont","words","world","would","wouldnt",
"your","youre","yours","yourself","yourselves"]

''' DEFINING PSEUDO CONSTANTS SECTION '''

# PSEUDO CONSTANTS,
# Feel Free to change the minimum and
# maximum name length
MIN_SIZE = 3      # Minimum length of a proper name
MAX_SIZE = 20     # Maximum length of a proper name

''' EXTRACT PROPER NAMES SECTION '''

def ExtractProperNames(theString, dictionary):
    ''' Input String to search,
        Output Dictionary of Proper Names
    '''

    # Extract each continuous string of characters

    wordList = theString.split()

    # Now, let's determine which words are possible
    # proper names and create a list of them.
    '''

    For this example words are considered possible
    proper names if they are:
    1) Title case
    2) Meet the minimum and maximum length criteria
    3) The word is NOT in the stop word list

    The Python built in string method string.istitle()
    is used to identify title case
```

```python
    ''' 

for eachWord in wordList:

    if eachWord.istitle() and len(eachWord) >=
        MIN_SIZE and len(eachWord) <= MAX_SIZE and
        eachWord.lower() not in STOP_WORDS:

        '''
        if the word meets the specified conditions
          it is added to the properNamesDictionary
        '''
        try:
            # if the word exists in the dictionary
              # then add 1 to the occurances
            cnt = properNamesDictionary[eachWord]
            properNamesDictionary[eachWord] =
                cnt + 1
        except:
            # If the word is not yet in the
              # dictionary
            # add it and set the number of
            # occurances to 1
            properNamesDictionary[eachWord] = 1
    else:
        # otherwise loop to the next possible word
        continue

# the function returns the created
#    properNamesDictionary

return properNamesDictionary
```

```python
# End Extract Proper Names Function

''' MAIN PROGRAM ENTRY SECTION '''

'''
Main program for Extract Proper Names
'''
if __name__ == "__main__":

    ''' Main Program Entry Point '''

    print("\nPython Proper Name Extraction ")
    print("Python Forensics, Inc. \n")
    print("Script Started", str(datetime.now()))
    print()

    # Create empty dictionary
    properNamesDictionary = {}

    for eachLine in sys.stdin:

        txt = re.sub("[^A-Za-z']", ' ', eachLine)

        '''
        Call the ExtractProperNames function
        which returns a Python dictionary of possible
        proper names along with the number of occurances
        of that name.

        This function performs all the heavy lifting
        of extracting out each possible proper name
        '''

        properNamesDictionary =
            ExtractProperNames(txt,
            properNamesDictionary)
```

```python
# Once all the standard input lines are read
# the value is the number of occurrences of the
# proper name

# This approach will print out the possible
# proper names with
# the highest occurrence first

'''

PRINT RESULTING POSSIBLE PROPER NAMES
SECTION '''

print()

for eachName in sorted(properNamesDictionary,
    key=properNamesDictionary.get, reverse=True):

    print('%4d' %
        properNamesDictionary[eachName],end="")

    print( '%20s' % eachName)

print("\n\nScript Ended", str(datetime.now()))
print()

# End Main Function
```

Executing the Combined PowerShell to Python ProperNames Scripts

The PowerShell script was then executed against a small directory of text files. The files were stored in the C:\PS\Text folder for ease of access. You can change the target folder variable $targetPath to modify the target folder. See Figure 6-5.

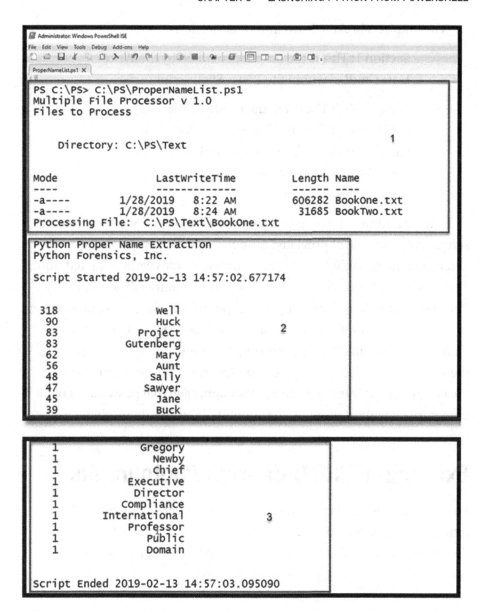

Figure 6-5. Resulting output PowerShell/Python combination (output reduced for brevity)

The output is broken down into three sections:

> Section 1: This is the output generated by the Write-Host CmdLet within the PowerShell script.
>
> Sections 2–3: These are the results generated by the Python script processing of the BookOne.txt. The output is repeated for BookTwo.txt as the PowerShell loops through all the text files found in the specified directory.

After examining the output of the combined PowerShell/Python scripts even with the abbreviated output, you will likely be able to determine the text that these possible proper names were extracted from. This is only one possibility of processing the content of files acquired by PowerShell and then delivering that output to Python for post-processing.

This combination provides a baseline model that can be duplicated for additional results. Also, by inserting Invoke-Command sequences in the PowerShell script, you can collect files and file contents throughout the enterprise. Now let's look at another approach that passes a list of file names to the Python script vs. the content of the files themselves.

Extracting EXIF Data from Photographs

For this example, the PowerShell script will be kept small and the heavy lifting will be off-loaded to the Python script where we will leverage key libraries to extract EXIF data including the geo-location information contained in the EXIF headers of JPEG images.

PowerShell Script

The PowerShell script in Figure 6-6 is broken down into four common elements with a slight twist.

1. Define a local variable $Python with the full path to the Python executable of your choice.

2. Define a local variable $Script that defines the full path to the Python script that will be executed.

3. Define a local variable $files that stores the set of files that match the search criteria *.jpg. The $jpegList local variable extracts the full path of each file and eliminates the headers leaving just the list of files that we intend to process.

4. This line passes the contents of the local variable $jpegList to the Python script. The key element here is the ampersand (&) that directs PowerShell to launch the external program. The Python script will receive each full pathname acquired by the PowerShell script, one per line passed via stdin.

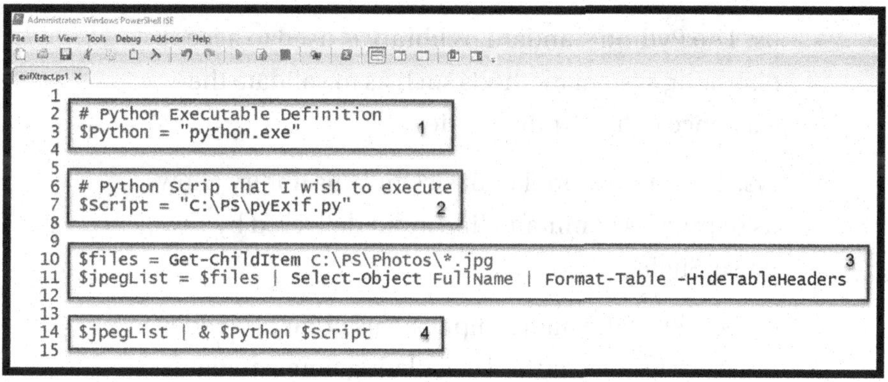

Figure 6-6. *PowerShell PhotoMap.ps1 script*

pyGeo.py Python Script

The Python script depicted in Listing 6-2 is broken down into eight major sections described here:

1. LIBRARY IMPORT

2. DEFINING PSEUDO CONSTANTS

3. EXTRACT GPS DICTIONARY

4. EXTRACT LATTITUDE AND LONGITUDE

5. CONVERT GPS COORDINATES TO DEGRESS

6. MAIN PROGRAM ENTRY

7. GENERATE RESULTS TABLE

8. GENERATE CSV FILE

LIBRARY IMPORT: As the name implies, this is where the needed Python libraries are loaded. They include:

- **os**: The Python standard os library is used to access operating system methods such as to validate the existence of files or directories.

- **sys**: As demonstrated in BasicOne, this library allows us to process command line input delivered by PowerShell.

- **datetime**: As the name implies, this library provides methods for display and calculating time and date details.

- **PIL**: The third-party Python Image library provides methods to access and extract EXIF data including geolocation information.

166

- prettytable: The third-party Python library provides the ability to tabularize data within a simple text-based table structure.

EXTRACT GPS DICTIONARY: This function is passed a filename to process, and verifies that the file is a valid image, and contains geolocation information. If it does, the geolocation information is collected, with GPS Dictionary and basic EXIF data is returned.

EXTRACT LATITUDE AND LONGITUDE: This function extracts the GPSLatitude and GPSLongitude and the associated reference from the GPS Dictionary provided. These values are not stored as degrees which most mapping programs require. Therefore, they are converted to degrees using the ConvertToDegress function. The orientation is then set accordingly. For example, if the latitude reference is South, then the latitude in degrees must be set to a negative value.

CONVERT TO DEGRESS: This function converts the GPS Coordinates stored in the EXIF data to degrees.

MAIN PROGRAM ENTRY: The main program first prints several heading messages. Then creates an empty picture list. Then as in the BasicOne.py example, the script processes each line from the system standard input provided by the PowerShell script. Each line contains the full path of files identified by the associated PowerShell script. Each filename is then appended to the picture list.

Next, an empty latLonList is created to hold the results of the GPS extraction from each picture. Each file is verified to exist, then the Extract GPS Dictionary is called. If the resulting GPS Dictionary contains data, the Extract Latitude Longitude function is called. Providing that valid latitude / longitude data is found, the base name of the file, the latitude and Longitude data are appended to the latLonList.

GENERATE RESULTS TABLE: The generate results table section produces a pretty table of results from the latLonList. Once the table is created, it is printed so the results of the extraction can be displayed in PowerShell.

GENERATE CSV FILE: Finally, the script generates a comma separated value (CSV) file LatLon.csv. This is formatted such that it can be imported into a Web-based mapping tool.

Listing 6-2. pyGeo.py Python Script

```
'''

EXIF Data Acquistion
January 2019
Version 1.1
'''


'''

Copyright (c) 2019 Chet Hosmer, Python Forensics

Permission is hereby granted, free of charge, to any person
obtaining a copy of this software and associated documentation
files (the "Software"), to deal in the Software without
restriction, including without limitation the rights to use,
copy, modify, merge, publish, distribute, sublicense, and/
or sell copies of the Software, and to permit persons to whom
the Software is furnished to do so, subject to the following
conditions:

The above copyright notice and this permission notice shall be
included in all copies or substantial
portions of the Software.

'''
# Usage Example:
# fileList | python pyExif.py
#
# Requirement: Python 3.x
#
```

```
# Requirement: 3rd Party Library that is
#               utilized is: PILLOW
#               to install PILLOW utilize the follow CMD
#               from the command line
#
#               pip install PILLOW
#
# The Script will extract the EXIF/GEO data from jpeg
# files piped into the script and generate tabular list # of
the extracted EXIF and geo location data along with # the
creation of a CSV file with LAT/LON Data
#

''' LIBRARY IMPORT SECTION '''
# Python Standard: Operating System Methods
import os

# Python Standard : System Methods
import sys

# Python Standard  datetime method from Standard Library
from datetime import datetime

# import the Python Image Library
# along with TAGS and GPS related TAGS
# Note you must install the PILLOW Module
# pip install PILLOW

from PIL import Image
from PIL.ExifTags import TAGS, GPSTAGS

# Import the PrettyTable Library to produce
# tabular results

from prettytable import PrettyTable
```

```python
''' EXTRACT GPS DICTIONARY SECTION '''

#
# Extract EXIF Data
#
# Input: Full Pathname of the target image
#
# Return: gps Dictionary and selected exifData list
#
def ExtractGPSDictionary(fileName):

    try:
        pilImage = Image.open(fileName)
        exifData = pilImage._getexif()

    except Exception:
        # If exception occurs from PIL processing
        # Report the
        return None, None

    # Interate through the exifData
    # Searching for GPS Tags

    imageTimeStamp = "NA"
    cameraModel = "NA"
    cameraMake = "NA"
    gpsData = False

    gpsDictionary = {}

    if exifData:

        for tag, theValue in exifData.items():

            # obtain the tag
            tagValue = TAGS.get(tag, tag)
```

```python
            # Collect basic image data if available

            if tagValue == 'DateTimeOriginal':
                imageTimeStamp =
                                exifData.get(tag).strip()

            if tagValue == "Make":
                cameraMake = exifData.get(tag).strip()

            if tagValue == 'Model':
                cameraModel = exifData.get(tag).strip()

            # check the tag for GPS
            if tagValue == "GPSInfo":

                gpsData = True;

                # Found it !
                # Use a Dictionary to hold the GPS Data

                # Loop through the GPS Information
                for curTag in theValue:
                    gpsTag = GPSTAGS.get(curTag, curTag)
                    gpsDictionary[gpsTag] =
                                    theValue[curTag]

        basicExifData = [imageTimeStamp,
                        cameraMake, cameraModel]

        return gpsDictionary, basicExifData

    else:
        return None, None

# End ExtractGPSDictionary ============================

''' EXTRACT LATTITUDE AND LONGITUDE SECTION '''

#
```

```python
# Extract the Lattitude and Longitude Values
# From the gpsDictionary
#

def ExtractLatLon(gps):

    # to perform the calcuation we need at least
    # lat, lon, latRef and lonRef

    try:
        latitude    = gps["GPSLatitude"]
        latitudeRef = gps["GPSLatitudeRef"]
        longitude   = gps["GPSLongitude"]
        longitudeRef = gps["GPSLongitudeRef"]

        lat = ConvertToDegrees(latitude)
        lon = ConvertToDegrees(longitude)

        # Check Latitude Reference
        # If South of the Equator then
        #     lat value is negative

        if latitudeRef == "S":
            lat = 0 - lat

        # Check Longitude Reference
        # If West of the Prime Meridian in
        # Greenwich then the Longitude value is negative

        if longitudeRef == "W":
            lon = 0- lon

        gpsCoor = {"Lat": lat,
                   "LatRef":latitudeRef,
                   "Lon": lon,
                   "LonRef": longitudeRef}
```

```
        return gpsCoor

    except:
        return None

# End Extract Lat Lon ======================================

''' CONVERT GPS COORDINATES TO DEGRESS '''

#
# Convert GPSCoordinates to Degrees
#
# Input gpsCoordinates value from in EXIF Format
#

def ConvertToDegrees(gpsCoordinate):

    d0 = gpsCoordinate[0][0]
    d1 = gpsCoordinate[0][1]
    try:
        degrees = float(d0) / float(d1)
    except:
        degrees = 0.0

    m0 = gpsCoordinate[1][0]
    m1 = gpsCoordinate[1][1]
    try:
        minutes = float(m0) / float(m1)
    except:
        minutes=0.0

    s0 = gpsCoordinate[2][0]
    s1 = gpsCoordinate[2][1]
    try:
```

```
        seconds = float(s0) / float(s1)
    except:
        seconds = 0.0

    floatCoordinate = float (degrees + (minutes / 60.0) +
    (seconds / 3600.0))

    return floatCoordinate

''' MAIN PROGRAM ENTRY SECTION '''

if __name__ == "__main__":
    '''

    pyExif Main Entry Point
    '''

    print("\nExtract EXIF Data from JPEG Files")
    print("Python Forensics, Inc. \n")

    print("Script Started", str(datetime.now()))
    print()

    ''' PROCESS PIPED DATA FROM POWERSHELL SECTION '''

    pictureList = []

    # Process data from standard input as a file list

    for eachLine in sys.stdin:
        entry = eachLine.strip()
        if entry:
            pictureList.append(entry)

    print("Processing Photos ...")
    print()

    # CDH
```

```python
# Created a mapping object

''' PROCESS EACH JPEG FILE SECTION '''

latLonList = []

for targetFile in pictureList:

    if os.path.isfile(targetFile):

        gpsDictionary, exifList = \
                ExtractGPSDictionary(targetFile)

        if exifList:
            TS = exifList[0]
            MAKE = exifList[1]
            MODEL = exifList[2]
        else:
            TS = 'NA'
            MAKE = 'NA'
            MODEL = 'NA'

        if (gpsDictionary != None):

            # Obtain the Lat Lon values from
            # the gpsDictionary
            #    Converted to degrees
            # The return value is a dictionary
            #    key value pairs

            dCoor = ExtractLatLon(gpsDictionary)

            if dCoor:
                lat = dCoor.get("Lat")
                latRef = dCoor.get("LatRef")
                lon = dCoor.get("Lon")
```

```python
                    lonRef = dCoor.get("LonRef")

                if ( lat and lon and
                      latRef and lonRef):

                    latLonList.append(
                      [os.path.basename(targetFile),
                      '{:4.4f}'.format(lat),
                      '{:4.4f}'.format(lon),
                      TS, MAKE, MODEL])

                else:
                    print("WARNING",
                            "No GPS EXIF Data for ",
                            targetFile)
            else:
                continue
        else:
            continue
    else:
        print("WARNING", " not a valid file", targetFile)

# Create Result Table Display using PrettyTable

''' GENERATE RESULTS TABLE SECTION '''

''' Result Table Heading '''
resultTable = PrettyTable(['File-Name',
                  'Lat','Lon',
                  'TimeStamp',
                  'Make', 'Model'])

for loc in latLonList:
```

```python
        resultTable.add_row( [loc[0], loc[1],
                              loc[2], loc[3],
                              loc[4], loc[5] ])

    resultTable.align = "l"
    print(resultTable.get_string(sortby="File-Name"))

    ''' GENERATE CSV FILE SECTION '''

    # Create Simple CSV File Result
    with open("LatLon.csv", "w") as outFile:
        # Write Heading
        outFile.write("Name, Lat, Long\n")

        # Process All entries and write
        # each line comma separated

        for loc in latLonList:
            outFile.write(loc[0]+","+
                          loc[1]+","+
                          loc[2]+"\n")

    print("LatLon.csv File Created Successfully")

    print("\nScript Ended", str(datetime.now()))
    print()
```

Executing the Combined PowerShell to Python exifxtract Scripts

The final step is to execute the PowerShell script which will pass the identified filenames to the Python script. The folder C:\PS\Photos contains a set of JPEG photographs to examine. By changing the $files variable in the PowerShell script, you can specify an alternative directory to examine. See Figure 6-7.

```
PS C:\PS> C:\PS\exifXtract.ps1

Extract EXIF Data from JPEG Files
Python Forensics, Inc.

Script Started 2019-02-14 10:15:07.017267

Processing Photos ...

+----------------+--------+----------+--------------------+--------+------------------------+
| File-Name      | Lat    | Lon      | TimeStamp          | Make   | Model                  |
+----------------+--------+----------+--------------------+--------+------------------------+
| Biking.jpg     | 33.8755 | -116.3016 | 2006:02:11 11:06:37 | Canon  | Canon PowerShot A80    |
| Castle.JPG     | 55.0073 | 11.9109  | 2012:06:09 12:42:24 | PENTAX | PENTAX K-5             |
| Cat.jpg        | 59.9248 | 10.6956  | 2008:08:05 20:59:32 | Canon  | Canon EOS 400D DIGITAL |
| CoastLine.JPG  | 33.8193 | -78.6704 | 2018:02:02 17:30:38 | Apple  | iPhone 7               |
| Deutchland.JPG | 47.9750 | 7.8297   | 2010:06:23 15:32:25 | Apple  | iPhone 3G              |
| Disney.jpg     | 28.4188 | -81.5810 | 2010:08:18 11:38:37 | Canon  | Canon EOS 1000D        |
| Farm.jpg       | 42.5012 | -83.2507 | 2009:03:14 13:46:34 | NIKON  | COOLPIX P6000          |
| Munich.JPG     | 48.1413 | 11.5767  | 2010:06:21 16:00:57 | Apple  | iPhone 3G              |
| Turtle.jpg     | 25.3384 | 34.7397  | 2008:05:08 16:55:58 | Canon  | Canon EOS 5D           |
+----------------+--------+----------+--------------------+--------+------------------------+
LatLon.csv File Created Successfully

Script Ended 2019-02-14 10:15:07.048502
```

Figure 6-7. *Execution of photoMap.ps1*

The script processed a sample directory with nine JPEG image files. The results included the table of filenames associated with extracted Lat/Lon values. The LatLon.csv file was also created. The resulting Lat/Lon results can be then imported into web resources such as Google Maps to provide a visual mapping of the results.

Summary

This chapter focused on the development of a model to execute Python scripts from PowerShell. The model used the standard PowerShell piping model to acquire specific data and provide the output to the specified Python scripts using the PowerShell piping method.

These examples focused on small PowerShell scripts that perform discrete acquisitions, and then ultimately used Python's rich capabilities to perform the heavy lifting to process the results.

This model provides a rich baseline for experimentation, acquisition, and combination of PowerShell and Python. In some ways, this model seems slightly more streamlined than the subprocess method used to execute PowerShell scripts from Python. Both have their place of course, whether to control and automate existing PowerShell scripts or to drive output from PowerShell to Python.

CHAPTER 7

Loose Ends and Future Considerations

Having developed two solid approaches for the integration of PowerShell and Python (i.e., Python subprocessing and PowerShell pipelining), there are a couple of loose ends and future considerations that need to be addressed.

Loose Ends

The first involves using the PowerShell Invoke-Command CmdLet without needing to respond to a login pop-up each time, as shown in Figure 7-1.

© Chet Hosmer 2019

C. Hosmer, *PowerShell and Python Together*, https://doi.org/10.1007/978-1-4842-4504-0_7

Figure 7-1. *Windows PowerShell credential request*

This can be accomplished by creating a new credential object using the PowerShell System Management Automation PSCredential system. Figure 7-2 shows a simple PowerShell script that acquires the system event log from the computer PLUTO, using the Remote-Admin user credentials. This requires only four steps:

1. Create two local PowerShell variables: $targetComputer (the computer name you wish to access) and $userName (the username on the remote computer).

2. Create a plaintext string, $password, with the password associated with the remote user. Note the password is blacked out here. When embedding passwords in PowerShell scripts, it is vital that you keep the script secure from unauthorized access.

3. This step contains two important parts:

   a. First, the plaintext password is converted to
      the secure string, $securePassword. The secure
      string created by the ConvertTo-SecureString
      CmdLet can then be utilized with other
      CmdLets or functions that require a parameter
      with the type SecureString.

   b. Next, the secure credential object, $credential, is
      created. This requires $userName and the newly
      created $securePassword as parameters.

4. Finally, the newly created $credential PowerShell
   variable can be passed as the -Credential parameter
   within the Invoke-Command CmdLet.

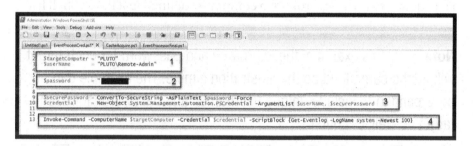

Figure 7-2. *PowerShell script to collect a remote event log with
embedded credentials*

Execution of the script acquires the system event log from the PLUTO
computer as shown in Figure 7-3. Note the output was truncated for
brevity.

```
PS C:\WINDOWS\system32> C:\PS\EventProcessCred.ps1

Index Time          EntryType   Source                  InstanceID Message                                              PSComputerName
----- ----          ---------   ------                  ---------- -------                                              --------------
 1074 Jan 29 15:34  Information Microsoft-Windows...             16 The description for Event ID '16' in Source 'Microsoft... PLUTO
 1073 Jan 29 15:34  Information Microsoft-Windows...             16 The description for Event ID '16' in Source 'Microsoft... PLUTO
 1072 Jan 29 15:26  Information Microsoft-Windows...             16 The description for Event ID '16' in Source 'Microsoft... PLUTO
 1071 Jan 29 13:40  Information Microsoft-Windows...             19 Installation Successful: Windows successfully installe... PLUTO
 1070 Jan 29 13:40  Information Microsoft-Windows...             43 Installation Started: Windows has started installing t... PLUTO
 1069 Jan 29 13:39  Information Microsoft-Windows...             44 Windows Update started downloading an update.         PLUTO
 1068 Jan 29 12:00  Information EventLog             2147489661 The system uptime is 346731 seconds.                  PLUTO
 1067 Jan 29 11:53  Information Microsoft-Windows...             19 Installation Successful: Windows successfully installe... PLUTO
 1066 Jan 29 11:52  Information Microsoft-Windows...             43 Installation Started: Windows has started installing t... PLUTO
 1065 Jan 29 11:52  Information Microsoft-Windows...             44 Windows Update started downloading an update.         PLUTO
 1064 Jan 29 11:22  Information Microsoft-Windows...             16 The description for Event ID '16' in Source 'Microsoft... PLUTO
 1063 Jan 28 23:41  Information Microsoft-Windows...              1 Possible detection of CVE: 2019-01-29T04:41:55.6987694... PLUTO
 1062 Jan 28 23:41  Information Microsoft-Windows...              1 Possible detection of CVE: 2019-01-29T04:41:55.6955383... PLUTO
```

Figure 7-3. *EventProcessCred.ps1 sample execution*

The second improvement leveraged the embedded credential
approach. The main reason for embedding credentials (beyond
convenience) is so that scripts can acquire data from multiple remote
computers from the same script without the requirement for interaction.
One method to accomplish this is to create a list of target computer names
to access. PowerShell lists are useful and can be used to loop through
multiple selections using the *foreach* operator. Figure 7-4 shows an example
that acquires system logs from two computers defined in a PowerShell list.

Note For this example, the username and password for each target
will be the same to keep the illustration simple. The example can
be expanded to include unique usernames and passwords for each
target as well, of course.

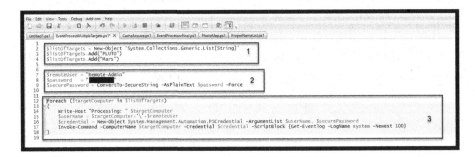

Figure 7-4. *Acquiring system event logs from multiple target
computers with embedded credentials*

This script is broken down into three steps:

1. This section creates a PowerShell object $listOfTargets which is a simple list of strings. Each string represents the name of a target computer. The newly created list has no elements. The $listOfTargets is then populated using the Add method that is associated with the PowerShell list object that was created.

2. The default $remoteUser variable is created and set to "Remote-Admin" which is the remote user Admin account that will be used. In addition, the $securePassword is created that will be used to access each remote target. Note the $credential is not created yet because it needs to be created uniquely for each target acquisition.

3. Finally, a loop is created that will do the following:

   a. Display the name of the Host being processed each time through the loop.

   b. Combine the current $targetComputer and the default $remoteUser name to create the unique $userName for this target. For example: **PLUTO\Remote-Admin.**

   c. Using the PowerShell System.Management. Automation capability, the unique $credential is then created each time through the loop, using the $userName and $securePassword PowerShell variables.

     d.   Then the Invoke-Command to acquire the system event log is executed with the current $targetComputer and the associated $credential required for access.

The abbreviated script output is shown in Figure 7-5.

```
PS C:\WINDOWS\system32> C:\PS\EventProcessMultipleTargets.ps1
Processing:  PLUTO

Index Time          EntryType   Source           InstanceID Message                                                PSComputerName
----- ----          ---------   ------           ---------- -------                                                --------------
 1089 Jan 29 21:42  Information Microsoft-windows...       19 Installation Successful: Windows successfully installe... PLUTO
 1088 Jan 29 21:42  Information Microsoft-windows...       43 Installation Started: Windows has started installing t... PLUTO
 1087 Jan 29 21:42  Information Microsoft-windows...       19 Installation Successful: Windows successfully installe... PLUTO
 1086 Jan 29 21:42  Information Microsoft-windows...       16 The description for Event ID '16' in Source 'Microsoft... PLUTO
 1085 Jan 29 21:42  Information Microsoft-windows...       43 Installation Started: Windows has started installing t... PLUTO
 1084 Jan 29 21:42  Information Microsoft-windows...       16 The description for Event ID '16' in Source 'Microsoft... PLUTO
 1083 Jan 29 21:42  Information Microsoft-windows...       16 The description for Event ID '16' in Source 'Microsoft... PLUTO
 1082 Jan 29 21:42  Information Microsoft-windows...       19 Installation Successful: Windows successfully installe... PLUTO
```

Figure 7-5. *Multiple target computer system event log execution*

Future Considerations

Integrating PowerShell and Python and combining two very powerful scripting environments has been a joy to work on. The research, experimentation, and model creation have been trying at times; however, the result is two viable and useful methods that will allow for the expansion of investigative solutions.

A rich basis for digital investigators can be found with the literally thousands of PowerShell CmdLets available to acquire material evidence from target computers locally or remotely. Combining that with the versatility and power of the Python environment brings forth the opportunity for boundless innovations and solutions.

Given these two models for integration, I challenge you to develop and expand new solutions that combine the best of both environments. I still think of PowerShell as a potent acquisition engine and Python as the backend analysis and processing component. However, that's only my view – you may have different ideas. So, run with those as well, the models provided here can support a wide range of possibilities.

Summary

This chapter focused on a couple of loose ends that will improve the automation aspects of PowerShell by embedding credentials with PowerShell scripts. This embedding enables multiple simultaneous acquisitions of evidence that can then be delivered to or driven by Python elements. This will certainly expand the reach of investigators and speed the acquisition and analysis of acquired evidence.

Good luck, and I look forward to communicating and collaborating on new investigative solutions that combine PowerShell and Python in unique ways.

APPENDIX A

Challenge Problem Solutions

The appendix contains solutions to several of the challenge problems presented in Chapter 1 through Chapter 5. Note that not all challenge problems are solved here as this is not meant to be a crossword puzzle cheat section. Rather, it provides key insights that will be needed to solve the challenges.

I firmly believe the only way to become proficient with Python, PowerShell, or the combination of both is to practice. One of the best ways to do this is to define a challenge you would like to solve, then start small and try different approaches. Then, and only then, integrate your experiments into scripts or programs. Note that this is slightly counter to traditional computer science approaches to waterfall or even spiral development; however, I believe this is the best way to learn. In one of my first books *Python Forensics*[1] I coined the phrase "test then code." At the time this was very fitting for the development of Python scripts, and I strongly believe that it still aligns well today for both PowerShell and Python.

---

[1]Syngress, 2014.

© Chet Hosmer 2019

C. Hosmer, *PowerShell and Python Together*, https://doi.org/10.1007/978-1-4842-4504-0

The appendix is broken down by chapter for easy reference.

Note   Just a reminder that many of the CmdLets and scripts require administrator privilege.

Chapter 1: Investigative CmdLets to Explore

Challenge One: Executing a "Find" Based on File Extension

```
PS C:\WINDOWS\system32> Get-Help Get-ChildItem
```

```
NAME
    Get-ChildItem
```

```
SYNOPSIS
    Gets the files and folders in a file system drive.
```

Example A: Find All Files with .jpg Extension

```
PS C:\WINDOWS\system32> get-childitem C:\ -include *.jpg
-recurse -force
```

```
Directory: C:\$Recycle.Bin\S-1-5-21-1545112040-36671619-
2396729391-1001\$RPSE7Z2\PHOTO
```

Mode	LastWriteTime	Length	Name
----	-------------	------	----
-a----	8/15/2018 11:24 AM	26903	20-fake-images-10.jpg
-a----	8/15/2018 11:21 AM	37651	20-fake-images-20.jpg

```
-a----          8/21/2018    8:01 AM        85175 area-51-
                                                  caller.jpg
-a----          7/30/2018    9:52 AM       177153 jets.JPG
-a----          8/21/2018    7:54 AM       137948 moon_landing_
                                                  hoax.jpg
```

Directory: C:\IMAGES

```
Mode                 LastWriteTime          Length Name
----                 -------------          ------ ----
-a----          9/3/2018     2:58 PM        624744 Biking.jpg
-a----          9/3/2018     2:58 PM       1224201 Castle.JPG
-a----          9/3/2018     2:58 PM        446759 Cat.jpg
-a----          9/3/2018     2:58 PM        600630 Deutchland.JPG
-a----          9/3/2018     2:58 PM        304930 Disney.jpg
-a----          9/3/2018     2:58 PM         96831 dscn0011.jpg
-a----          9/3/2018     2:58 PM         98012 kinderscout.jpg
-a----          9/3/2018     2:58 PM        252607 Munich.JPG
-a----          9/3/2018     2:58 PM       3352190 Rome.jpg
-a----          9/3/2018     2:58 PM         91329 Turtle.jpg
-a----          9/3/2018     2:58 PM          5459 zzz.jpg
```

--- OUTPUT truncated for brevity

Example B: Display Hidden System Files in C:\

```
PS C:\WINDOWS\system32> Get-ChildItem c:\ -Hidden -System
```

Directory: C:\

```
Mode                 LastWriteTime          Length Name
----                 -------------          ------ ----
d--hs-          2/5/2017     1:43 PM               $Recycle.Bin
d--hs-          1/21/2019    4:09 PM               Config.Msi
d--hsl          2/5/2017     1:49 PM               Documents and
                                                   Settings
```

d--hs-	1/31/2019	8:05 AM		System Volume Information
-arhs-	7/16/2016	7:43 AM	384322	bootmgr
-a-hs-	7/16/2016	7:43 AM	1	BOOTNXT
-a-hs-	1/12/2019	11:32 AM	5111406592	hiberfil.sys
-a-hs-	1/28/2019	11:20 PM	3891789824	pagefile.sys
-a-hs-	12/20/2018	1:56 PM	268435456	swapfile.sys

Challenge Two: Examining Network Settings

Example A: Get Basic TCP Network Settings

```
PS C:\WINDOWS\system32> Get-Help Get-NetIPConfiguration

NAME
    Get-NetIPConfiguration

SYNOPSIS
    Gets IP network configuration.

PS C:\WINDOWS\system32> Get-NetIPConfiguration -All


InterfaceAlias       : Ethernet
InterfaceIndex       : 8
InterfaceDescription : Realtek PCIe GBE Family Controller
NetProfile.Name      : hoz  3
IPv4Address          : 192.168.86.36
IPv6DefaultGateway   :
IPv4DefaultGateway   : 192.168.86.1
DNSServer            : 192.168.86.1
```

Example B: Get Current TCP Connections

```
PS C:\WINDOWS\system32> Get-NetTCPConnection | select-object
-Property LocalAddress, RemoteAddress, State, OwningProcess |
Format-Table -AutoSize
```

LocalAddress	RemoteAddress	State	OwningProcess
192.168.86.36	52.114.74.45	Established	67228
192.168.86.36	162.125.9.3	CloseWait	132676
192.168.86.36	162.125.33.7	CloseWait	132676
192.168.86.36	23.32.68.10	Established	156280
192.168.86.36	162.125.18.133	Established	132676
192.168.86.36	162.125.34.129	Established	132676
192.168.86.36	162.125.9.7	CloseWait	132676
192.168.86.36	17.249.156.16	Established	17736
192.168.86.36	162.125.18.133	Established	132676
192.168.86.36	162.125.9.4	CloseWait	132676
192.168.86.36	162.125.34.129	Established	132676

Challenge Three: Examining Firewall Settings

Example A: Check the Current Local Firewall State

```
PS C:\WINDOWS\system32> get-Help Get-NetFirewallProfile

NAME
    Get-NetFirewallProfile

SYNOPSIS
    Displays settings that apply to the per-profile configurations
    of the Windows Firewall with Advanced Security.

PS C:\WINDOWS\system32> Get-NetFirewallProfile | Select-Object
-Property Enabled, Profile
```

```
Enabled Profile
------- -------
   True Domain
   True Private
   True Public
```

Chapter 2: CmdLet Experimentation

In Chapter 2, the Start and Stop Transcript CmdLets will be used to capture the results of each CmdLet output. The resulting transcript is included at the end of this section with a selection of CmdLets that were experimented with.

```
PS C:\WINDOWS\system32> Get-Help Start-Transcript

NAME
    Start-Transcript

SYNOPSIS
    Creates a record of all or part of a Windows PowerShell
    session to a text file.

PS C:\WINDOWS\system32> Get-Help Stop-Transcript

NAME
    Stop-Transcript

SYNOPSIS
    Stops a transcript.

PS C:\WINDOWS\system32> Start-Transcript c:\PS\Transcript\
transcript.txt

Transcript started, output file is c:\PS\Transcript\transcript.
txt
```

Transcript of Commands and Responses

Note: Some output was abbreviated.

```
*********************
Windows PowerShell transcript start
Start time: 20190131103013
Username: PYTHON-3\cdhsl
RunAs User: PYTHON-3\cdhsl
Configuration Name:
Machine: PYTHON-3 (Microsoft Windows NT 10.0.17134.0)
Host Application: C:\WINDOWS\system32\WindowsPowerShell\v1.0\
PowerShell_ISE.exe
Process ID: 41620
PSVersion: 5.1.17134.407
PSEdition: Desktop
PSCompatibleVersions: 1.0, 2.0, 3.0, 4.0, 5.0, 5.1.17134.407
BuildVersion: 10.0.17134.407
CLRVersion: 4.0.30319.42000
WSManStackVersion: 3.0
PSRemotingProtocolVersion: 2.3
SerializationVersion: 1.1.0.1
*********************

Transcript started, output file is c:\PS\Transcript\transcript.txt

PS C:\WINDOWS\system32> Get-Process -ComputerName .
```

Handles	NPM(K)	PM(K)	WS(K)	CPU(s)	Id	SI	ProcessName
470	22	6524	4172	2,793.53	55708	2	AdobeCollabSync
277	14	2692	708	0.17	56592	2	AdobeCollabSync
238	23	9184	156	0.23	113824	2	ApplePhoto Streams
487	28	19988	22108	14.77	79164	2	Application FrameHost
166	9	2084	100	0.09	183548	2	AppVShNotify
157	8	1804	104	0.02	209908	0	AppVShNotify
375	25	5160	2020	2.17	17736	2	APSDaemo
1326	74	232108	173896	43.73	184112	2	POWERPNT
1210	86	380800	397292	240.86	41620	2	powershell_ise
941	91	50384	10732	3.31	166420	0	PRSvc
307	28	31836	1536	1.66	35788	2	QtWebEngine Process
339	15	6444	3408	3.67	12076	2	RAVBg64
345	16	7136	4712	3.77	23452	2	RAVBg64
608	26	19760	1536	0.41	6204	0	RealSenseDCM
0	14	1388	20876	167.36	96	0	Registry
449	20	10136	15780	9.48	17068	2	RemindersServer
220	9	1792	160	0.08	2540	0	RtkAudio Service64
126	9	1532	528	0.05	216496	2	rundll32
120	7	1384	6136	0.00	168436	0	SearchFilterHost
1241	83	57844	54048	52.45	161508	0	SearchIndexer
52	3	504	208	0.41	452	0	smss
220	13	5172	5116	223.39	2364	0	svchost
155	9	1696	424	0.09	14104	2	TUAuto Reactivator64

329	20	6296	11196	851.14	60052	2	TuneUpUtilities App64
1167	34	46024	32928	12,831.14	63708	0	TuneUpUtilities Service64
198	14	2912	3408	2.34	4224	0	UploaderService
124	8	1400	316	0.52	15912	2	WavesSvc64
110	8	2624	156	0.02	4380	0	WavesSysSvc64
156	10	1528	36	0.02	724	0	wininit
247	10	2668	2528	3.83	215952	2	winlogon
1754	91	200124	197816	415.23	67228	2	WINWORD
343	14	15340	13956	971.41	15696	0	WmiPrvSE
308	17	11144	8360	319.03	24228	0	WmiPrvSE
237	10	2348	764	0.61	132372	0	WUDFHost

```
PS C:\WINDOWS\system32> Get-Process -Name chrome
```

Handles	NPM(K)	PM(K)	WS(K)	CPU(s)	Id	SI	ProcessName
271	21	18696	24180	0.16	26420	2	chrome
338	32	94600	49056	11.11	48132	2	chrome
273	25	36024	36760	1.44	76284	2	chrome
558	30	92792	67576	26.75	83340	2	chrome
343	30	80788	87232	3.33	88260	2	chrome
266	19	13940	17364	0.08	115852	2	chrome
142	11	1988	7236	0.05	128480	2	chrome
356	33	97140	78868	3.84	128952	2	chrome
223	10	2100	7252	0.03	148004	2	chrome
267	21	21652	23044	0.25	149520	2	chrome
273	22	26964	26600	0.30	197144	2	chrome
1639	73	115292	110896	64.27	214792	2	chrome

```
PS C:\WINDOWS\system32> Get-MpThreat
None reported

PS C:\WINDOWS\system32> get-service | where-object {$_.Status
-eq "Stopped"}

Status    Name                DisplayName
------    ----                -----------
Stopped   AJRouter            AllJoyn Router Service
Stopped   ALG                 Application Layer Gateway Service
Stopped   AppIDSvc            Application Identity
Stopped   AppReadiness        App Readiness
Stopped   AppVClient          Microsoft App-V Client
Stopped   AppXSvc             AppX Deployment Service (AppXSVC)
Stopped   AssignedAccessM...  AssignedAccessManager Service
Stopped   AxInstSV            ActiveX Installer (AxInstSV)
Stopped   BcastDVRUserSer...  GameDVR and Broadcast User
                              Service_...
Stopped   BDESVC              BitLocker Drive Encryption Service
Stopped   BluetoothUserSe...  Bluetooth User Support
                              Service_2a63...
Stopped   Bonjour Service     Bonjour Service
Stopped   CaptureService_...  CaptureService_2a637185
Stopped   CertPropSvc         Certificate Propagation
Stopped   ssh-agent           OpenSSH Authentication Agent
Stopped   SupportAssistAgent  Dell SupportAssist Agent
Stopped   svsvc               Spot Verifier
Stopped   swprv               Microsoft Software Shadow Copy
                              Prov...
Stopped   TermService         Remote Desktop Services
Stopped   TieringEngineSe...  Storage Tiers Management
Stopped   TrustedInstaller    Windows Modules Installer
Stopped   tzautoupdate        Auto Time Zone Updater
```

```
Stopped  UevAgentService       User Experience Virtualization
                               Service
Stopped  UmRdpService          Remote Desktop Services UserMode
                               Po...
Stopped  upnphost              UPnP Device Host
Stopped  VacSvc                Volumetric Audio Compositor Service
Stopped  vds                   Virtual Disk
Stopped  VMAuthdService        VMware Authorization Service
Stopped  vmicguestinterface    Hyper-V Guest Service Interface
Stopped  vmicheartbeat         Hyper-V Heartbeat Service
Stopped  vmickvpexchange       Hyper-V Data Exchange Service
Stopped  vmicrdv               Hyper-V Remote Desktop
                               Virtualizati...
Stopped  vmicshutdown          Hyper-V Guest Shutdown Service
Stopped  vmictimesync          Hyper-V Time Synchronization
                               Service
Stopped  vmicvmsession         Hyper-V PowerShell Direct Service
Stopped  vmicvss               Hyper-V Volume Shadow Copy
                               Requestor
Stopped  VMnetDHCP             VMware DHCP Service
Stopped  VMUSBArbService       VMware USB Arbitration Service
Stopped  VMware NAT Service    VMware NAT Service

PS C:\WINDOWS\system32> Get-Location

Path
----
C:\WINDOWS\system32

PS C:\WINDOWS\system32> Set-Location C:\PS
```

PS C:\PS> **Test-NetConnection**

```
ComputerName          : internetbeacon.msedge.net
RemoteAddress         : 13.107.4.52
InterfaceAlias        : Ethernet
SourceAddress         : 192.168.86.36
PingSucceeded         : True
PingReplyDetails (RTT) : 24 ms
```

PS C:\PS> **Get-Disk | Format-List ***

```
DiskNumber            : 0
PartitionStyle        : GPT
ProvisioningType      : Fixed
OperationalStatus     : Online
HealthStatus          : Healthy
BusType               : SATA
UniqueIdFormat        : FCPH Name
OfflineReason         :
UniqueId              : 5000039751D8A26D
AdapterSerialNumber   :
AllocatedSize         : 1000203837440
BootFromDisk          : True
FirmwareVersion       : AXOP3D
FriendlyName          : TOSHIBA MQ01ABD100
Guid                  : {ea267102-e3e3-4a17-b349-e5e0161bc012}
IsBoot                : True
IsClustered           : False
IsHighlyAvailable     : False
IsOffline             : False
IsReadOnly            : False
IsScaleOut            : False
IsSystem              : True
```

```
LargestFreeExtent      : 1048576
Location               : Integrated : Adapter 0 : Port 0
LogicalSectorSize      : 512
Manufacturer           :
Model                  : TOSHIBA MQ01ABD100
Number                 : 0
NumberOfPartitions     : 6
Path                   : \\?\scsi#disk&ven_toshiba&prod_mq01abd1
                         00#4&1b6d0cbc&0&000000#{53f56307-b6bf-
                         11d0-94f2-00a0c91efb8b}
PhysicalSectorSize     : 4096
SerialNumber           :             X6LSTAXNT
Signature              :
Size                   : 1000204886016
PSComputerName         :
CimClass               : ROOT/Microsoft/Windows/Storage:MSFT_
                         Disk
CimInstanceProperties  : {ObjectId, PassThroughClass,
                         PassThroughIds,
                         PassThroughNamespace...}
CimSystemProperties    : Microsoft.Management.Infrastructure.
                         CimSystemProperties
DiskNumber             : 2
PartitionStyle         : MBR
ProvisioningType       : Fixed
OperationalStatus      : Online
HealthStatus           : Healthy
BusType                : USB
UniqueIdFormat         : Vendor Specific
OfflineReason          : USBSTOR\DISK&VEN_DYMO&PROD_PNP&REV_1.00\
                         7&347EDADD&0&15314622032011&0:PYTHON-3
```

```
AdapterSerialNumber    :
AllocatedSize          : 4193792
BootFromDisk           : False
FirmwareVersion        : 1.00
FriendlyName           : DYMO PnP
Guid                   :
IsBoot                 : False
IsClustered            : False
IsHighlyAvailable      : False
IsOffline              : False
IsReadOnly             : False
IsScaleOut             : False
IsSystem               : False
LargestFreeExtent      : 0
Location               : Integrated : Adapter 0 : Port 0
LogicalSectorSize      : 512
Manufacturer           : DYMO
Model                  : PnP
Number                 : 2
NumberOfPartitions     : 1
PhysicalSectorSize     : 512
SerialNumber           : 15314622032011
Signature              : 6975421
Size                   : 4193792
PSComputerName         :
CimClass               : ROOT/Microsoft/Windows/Storage:MSFT_
                         Disk
CimInstanceProperties  : {ObjectId, PassThroughClass,
                         PassThroughIds,
                         PassThroughNamespace...}
```

```
CimSystemProperties    : Microsoft.Management.Infrastructure.
                         CimSystemProperties
PS C:\PS> Stop-Transcript
**********************
Windows PowerShell transcript end
End time: 20190131103856
**********************
```

Chapter 3: Create File Inventory List with Hashes

```
#
# Simple file Inventory Script
#

# Function to convert size values to human readable
function GetMBSize($num)
{
    $suffix = "MB"
    $MB = 1048576

    $num = $num / $MB


    "{0:N2} {1}" -f $num, $suffix
}

# Set Report Title
$rptTitle = "File Inventory"
# Get the current date and tme
$rptDate=Get-Date

# Set the target Directory and parameters
$targetDirectory = "c:\"
```

```powershell
# Create HTML Header Section
$Header = @"
<style>
TABLE {border-width: 1px; border-style: solid; border-color:
black; border-collapse: collapse;}
TD {border-width: 1px; padding: 3px; border-style: solid;
border-color: black;}
</style>
<p>
<b> $rptTitle</b>
<p>
<b> Date: $rptDate </b>
<p>
<b> Target: $targetDirectory </b>
<p>
"@

# Provide script output for user
Write-Host "Create Simple File Inventory"

$dir = Get-ChildItem $targetDirectory -File

# Create an empty array to hold values
$outArray = @()

# Loop through each file found
foreach ($item in $dir)
{
    # create and object to hold item values from separate
    CmdLets
    $tempObj = "" | Select "FileName", "Attribute", "Size",
    "HashValue"
```

```
    # Get the fullname including path
    $fullName  = $item.FullName

    # Get the attributes assoicated with this file
    $attributes = $item.Attributes
    $size       = GetMBSize($item.Length)

    # Generate the SHA-256 Hash of the file
    $hashObj = Get-FileHash $fullName -ErrorAction Silently
    Continue
    # Get just the Hash Value
    $hashValue = $hashObj.Hash

    # if hash value could not be generated set to Not Available
    if ([string]::IsNullOrEmpty($hashValue))
    {
        $hashValue = "Not Available"
    }

    # Fill in the tempObj
    $tempObj.FileName  = $fullName
    $tempObj.Attribute = $attributes
    $tempObj.Size      = $size
    $tempObj.HashValue = $hashValue

    # Add the tempObj to the outArray
    $outArray += $tempObj

    # Clear the output array
    $tempObj = $null
}

$outArray | ConvertTo-Html -Head $Header -Property FileName,
Attribute, Size, HashValue |
 Out-File test.html
```

```
#$outArray | ConvertTo-Html | out-file test.html
Write-Host "Script Completed"
Write-Host "test.html created"
```

Sample PowerShell Script Output

```
PS C:\PS> C:\PS\testInventory.ps1
Create Simple File Inventory
Scan the C: Drive for Hidden and System Files Only
Script Completed
test.html created

PS C:\PS>
```

HTML Screenshots

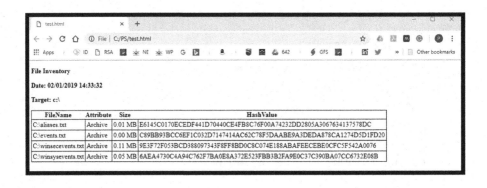

Note   By adding the -System argument to the Get-ChildItem command, you would obtain the system files in the c:\ directory.

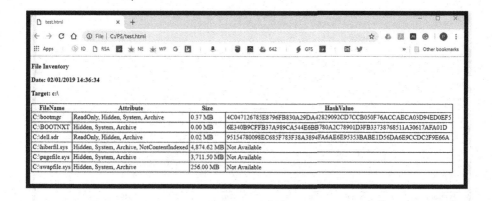

Note   By changing the script $targetFolder and adding the -Recurse to the Get-ChildItem command, you can process the entire C:\ drive. Running the script against the c:\PS\ folder including the -Recurse Parameter we get the following result (truncated for brevity).

Note   By changing the $MB variable to $KB = 1024 you can then produce results in Kilobytes, modify the script, and give that a try.

207

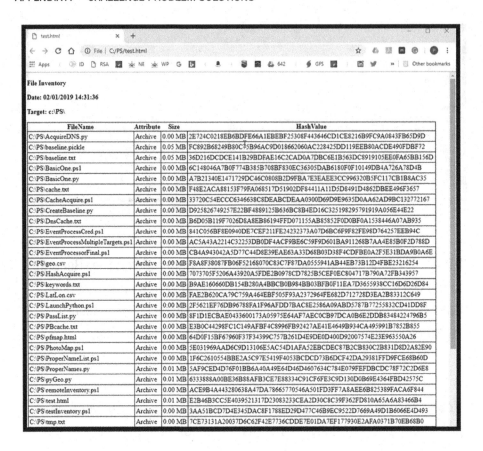

Also, utilizing the Invoke-Command CmdLet, you can extend this example to collect file inventories of remote systems.

Chapter 4: Perform Remote Script Execution

Remote PowerShell Command Execution directly from Python:

Example A: Acquire Remote Processes from PLUTO

```
import subprocess
runningProcess = subprocess.check_output("PowerShell
-Executionpolicy byPass
                -Command Invoke-Command -ComputerName PLUTO
-Credential PLUTO\Remote-Admin -ScriptBlock {Get-Process}")

print runningProcess.decode()
```

Sample Execution

```
Python Shell   Debug I/O   Search   Exceptions   Search in Files   Stack Data

Commands execute without debug. Use arrow keys for history.                                                              ☀ ☰ Options
>>>
>>> runningProcess = subprocess.check_output("PowerShell -Executionpolicy byPass -Command Invoke-Command -ComputerName PL
>>> print runningProcess.decode()

Handles  NPM(K)    PM(K)     WS(K)    CPU(s)ᴵ   Id  SI ProcessName                    PSComputerName
-------  ------    -----     -----    ------    --  -- -----------                    --------------
    403      23    12712     23348      0.88  1860   1 ApplicationFrameHost           PLUTO
    333      15     2924      3448      0.27  4608   1 browser_broker                 PLUTO
    375      14     1556      2008      4.14   372   0 csrss                          PLUTO
    360      15     1676      2096      1.52   448   1 csrss                          PLUTO
    394      16     4040      8496      1.17  2952   1 ctfmon                         PLUTO
    431      19     5724     10684      2.97  1852   0 dasHost                        PLUTO
     81       5      900      1136      0.05  2612   0 dasHost                        PLUTO
    130       7     1456      5776            2768   0 dllhost                        PLUTO
    126       8     1500      5544      0.17  3464   1 dllhost                        PLUTO
    222      16     3288      6244      0.52  5648   1 dllhost                        PLUTO
    754      44    37780     39720      5.16   848   1 dwm                            PLUTO
   1770      67    31700     61356     38.66  1504   1 explorer                       PLUTO
     49       7     1836      2164      0.22   676   1 fontdrvhost                    PLUTO
     49       6     1396      1392      0.05   684   0 fontdrvhost                    PLUTO
```

Example B: Acquire Remote Services from PLUTO

```
import subprocess
runningServices = subprocess.check_output("PowerShell
-Executionpolicy byPass
              -Command Invoke-Command -ComputerName PLUTO
-Credential PLUTO\Remote-Admin -ScriptBlock {Get-Service}")

print runningServices.decode()
```

```
Python Shell   Debug I/O   Search   Exceptions   Search in Files   Stack Data

Commands execute without debug. Use arrow keys for history.                                    ☀ ⊞  Options ▼

>>> runningServices = subprocess.check_output("PowerShell -Executionpolicy byPass -Comman
>>> print runningServices.decode()

    Status   Name I                DisplayName                                  PSComputerName
    ------   ----                  -----------                                  --------------
    Stopped  AJRouter              AllJoyn Router Service                       PLUTO
    Stopped  ALG                   Application Layer Gateway Service            PLUTO
    Stopped  AppIDSvc              Application Identity                         PLUTO
    Running  Appinfo               Application Information                      PLUTO
    Stopped  AppMgmt               Application Management                       PLUTO
    Stopped  AppReadiness          App Readiness                                PLUTO
    Stopped  AppVClient            Microsoft App-V Client                       PLUTO
    Stopped  AppXSvc               AppX Deployment Service (AppXSVC)            PLUTO
    Stopped  AssignedAccessM...    AssignedAccessManager Service                PLUTO
    Running  AudioEndpointBu...    Windows Audio Endpoint Builder               PLUTO
    Running  Audiosrv              Windows Audio                                PLUTO
    Stopped  AxInstSV              ActiveX Installer (AxInstSV)                 PLUTO
    Stopped  BcastDVRUserSer...    GameDVR and Broadcast User Service_....      PLUTO
    Stopped  BDESVC                BitLocker Drive Encryption Service           PLUTO
```

Example C: Acquire Remote IP Configuration from PLUTO

import subprocess

ipConfig = subprocess.check_output("PowerShell -Executionpolicy byPass

                   -Command Invoke-Command -ComputerName PLUTO

-Credential PLUTO\Remote-Admin -ScriptBlock { Get-NetIP

Configuration -All}")

print ipConfig.decode()

```
Python Shell   Debug I/O   Search   Exceptions   Search in Files   Stack Data
Commands execute without debug. Use arrow keys for history.                                          ⊕ ⊟  Options ▾
>>> ipConfig = subprocess.check_output("PowerShell -Executionpolicy byPass -Command Invoke-Command -ComputerName PLUTO -Credent:
>>> print ipConfig.decode()

    PSComputerName       : PLUTO
    RunspaceId           : f68fdf8c-7738-4dd8-b202-9113ad8f59a6
    ComputerName         : PLUTO
    InterfaceAlias       : Ethernet
    InterfaceIndex       : 9
    InterfaceDescription : Intel(R) PRO/1000 MT Desktop Adapter
    CompartmentId        : 1
    NetAdapter           : MSFT_NetAdapter (CreationClassName = "MSFT_NetAdapter", DeviceID =
                           "{9604506C-3293-40A8-8C15-D0249B141841}", SystemCreationClassName = "CIM_NetworkPort",
                           SystemName = "PLUTO")
    NetCompartment       : MSFT_NetCompartment (InstanceID = ";55;")
    NetIPv6Interface     : MSFT_NetIPInterface (Name = "C55??55;", CreationClassName = "", SystemCreationClassName = "",
                           SystemName = "")
    NetIPv4Interface     : MSFT_NetIPInterface (Name = "C55?55;", CreationClassName = "", SystemCreationClassName = "",
                           SystemName = "")
    NetProfile           : MSFT_NetConnectionProfile (InstanceID = "{9604506C-3293-40A8-8C15-D0249B141841}")
    AllIPAddresses       : {MSFT_NetIPAddress (Name = ";C?8;@8B8@8??55C55;55;", CreationClassName = "",
                           SystemCreationClassName = "", SystemName = ""), MSFT_NetIPAddress (Name =
                           "poB:DD?m?oD?p:BD?;C:Dn?@?/C55C55;55;", CreationClassName = "", SystemCreationClassName = "",
                           SystemName = "")}
    IPv6Address          : {}
    IPv6TemporaryAddress : {}
    IPv6LinkLocalAddress : {MSFT_NetIPAddress (Name = "poB:DD?m?oD?p:BD?;C:Dn?@?/C55C55;55;", CreationClassName = "",
                           SystemCreationClassName = "", SystemName = "")}
```

Chapter 5: Multiple Target Computer DNSCache Acquisition

Examining the scripts given in Chapter 6 provides the needed methods necessary to complete and advance this challenge. I challenge you to complete this one entirely on your own.

Index

A

argparse library, 108

B

[-b] baselineFile, 109

C

Client DNS cache data, 144
CmdLet experimentation,
        commands and
        responses, 194–203
CmdLet pipelining
    challenge problem, 41–43
    Format-Table, 25–26
    Get-Help, 26, 37–38
    Get-Process (*see* Get-Process)
    Get-Service, 23–26
    PowerShell transcript, 39–41
    Resolve-DnsName, 36–37
    Start-Transcript, 37–39
    Where-Object, 24
CmdLets investigation
    find execution
        hidden files, 191
        .jpg extension, 190–191

firewall settings,
        local state, 193–194
        network settings, TCP, 192, 193
Command-Information-Model
        (CIM), 3
Common-Object-Model (COM), 3

D

Disable-PSRemoting cmdlets, 124
Distributed Component Object
        Model (DCOM), 121
DNS CACHE SEARCHING, 143
DNS Client cache/DNS resolver
        cache, 126
Doman Name System (DNS), 126

E

Enable-PSRemoting
    cmdlet, 122–123
    Get-Help, 122
    Windows PowerShell
        remoting, 123
    WinRM service, 124, 126
Enable-PSRemoting cmdlet, 122
Enter-PSSession cmdlet, 80

© Chet Hosmer 2019
C. Hosmer, *PowerShell and Python Together*, https://doi.org/10.1007/978-1-4842-4504-0

EventProcessor
    EventLog CmdLets, 47–48
    Get-Help, 62–66
    HTML report file, 67–68
    script execution, 66
EXIF data extraction
    photoMap.ps1, extraction, 178
    PowerShell script, 164
    pyGeo.py Python Script, 166

F

File Inventory List, Hashes, 203–205
    HTML, 206–208
    PowerShell Script, 206
foreach operator, 184

G

Get-DNSClientCache
    Cmdlet, 128
    Google home page,
        navigation, 127
    TimeToLive property, 129–130
Get-Process
    automatic variables, 27–28
    -ExpandProperty command, 29
    ForEach-Object, 34
    Get-Help, 31–32
    Get-NetTCPConnections, 30–32
    Name Chrome command, 28–29
    OwningProcess, 32–33
    Process ID, 29–30

    remote IP addresses, 36–37
    Single Pipeline Solution, 34–36
    variables, 27

H

hitList variable, 143
-h option, 108

I, J, K

Integrated Scripting Environment
    (ISE), 3
Interactive shell, 102
Invoke-Command CmdLet, 133, 144

L, M

Loose ends
    EventProcessCred.ps1, 184
    Invoke-Command CmdLet, 181
    PowerShell credential
        request, 182
    system event log, 183, 186

N, O

-Name Parameter, 14

P, Q

PowerShell
    evolution, 2
    ISE, 3

Python, 2
PowerShell CacheAquire script
  AcquireDNS.py, 136–139
  argument parsing, 141
  dns cache searching, 143
  DNS remote, 143
  library import, 140
  loading keywords, 142
PowerShell CmdLets, 7–8
  Get-Help services, 9–11
  Get-Member, 14, 16–17
  Get-Process, 11–14
PowerShell execution, 142
PowerShell pipelining, *see* CmdLet
    pipelining
PowerShell scripts
  basic facts, 46
  CacheAcquire, 132
  cache.txt file, 134–135
  challenge problem, 51, 85–86
  CmdLet pipeline execution, 61–62
  .description section, 56–57
  DNS cache, 135
  EventProcessor (*see*
      EventProcessor)
  example section, 57–58
  Get-EventLog, 49–50
  local variable section, 60–61
  parameter, 57, 59–60, 133
  remote access, 68–69
  script header, 56
  .synopsis section, 56
  USB device (*see* USB device)

Proper names, extraction
  forensic investigation, 151
  PowerShell/Python
      combination, 162–164
  PowerShell script, 151–152
  Python script, 153–162
[-p] targetPath, 109
Python
  argument parsing, 108–109
  baseline.txt file, 102
  challenge problem, 118–119
  CmdLet, 94–95
  CreateBaseLine Python
      Script, 104–108, 110
  dictionary creation, 109
  HashAcquire.ps1 PowerShell
      script, 102, 110
  HashAquire.ps1 PowerShell
      Script, 99–102
  library import, 107
  main section, 109
  PowerShell command, 95–96
  pickle.load() method, 115–116
  pipeline command, 98–99
  PowerShell, 91–93, 117–118
  Powershell execution, 109
  run() method, 109
  subprocess.check_output()
      method, 95, 96
  TestDictDiff() function, 116
  TestDictEquality() function, 116
  VerifyBaseline.py script, 110–117
  WingIDE, 92–93, 97

Python script
  ExtractProperNamesFunction, 154
  library import, 153
  pseudo constants, 154
  Python ProperNames.py
      Script, 155–159, 161–162
  stop words list, 154

R

Remote Access method, 75
Remote Invocation,
      Get-DnsClientCache, 130–131
Remote Procedure Calls (RPCs), 121
Remote Script execution
  remote IP, PLUTO, 211–212
  remote processes, PLUTO, 209
  remote services, PLUTO, 210
Reversing roles, PowerShell
      script, 148
  EXIF data, extraction (*see* EXIF
      data extraction)
  Proper names extraction (*see*
      Proper names, extraction)
  Python script, 149–150

S

SkipNetworkProfileCheck
      parameter, 123
Start-Transcript, 37–39
-System argument, 206

T

[-t] tmpFile, 109

U, V

USB device
  Get-ItemProperty, 72–74
  Invoke-Command, 75–79, 81
  registry history, 70–71
  remote computer, 75
  USBAcquire script, 82–85

W, X, Y, Z

Windows Management Interface
      (WMI), 3
WingIDE, 92–93, 97
WS-Management technology, 122

Printed in the United States
By Bookmasters

Printed in the United States
By Bookmasters